AF270642

THE CAMPING AND HIKING ENCYCLOPEDIA

BY KATHRYN HULICK

Encyclopedias

An Imprint of Abdo Reference
abdobooks.com

TABLE OF CONTENTS

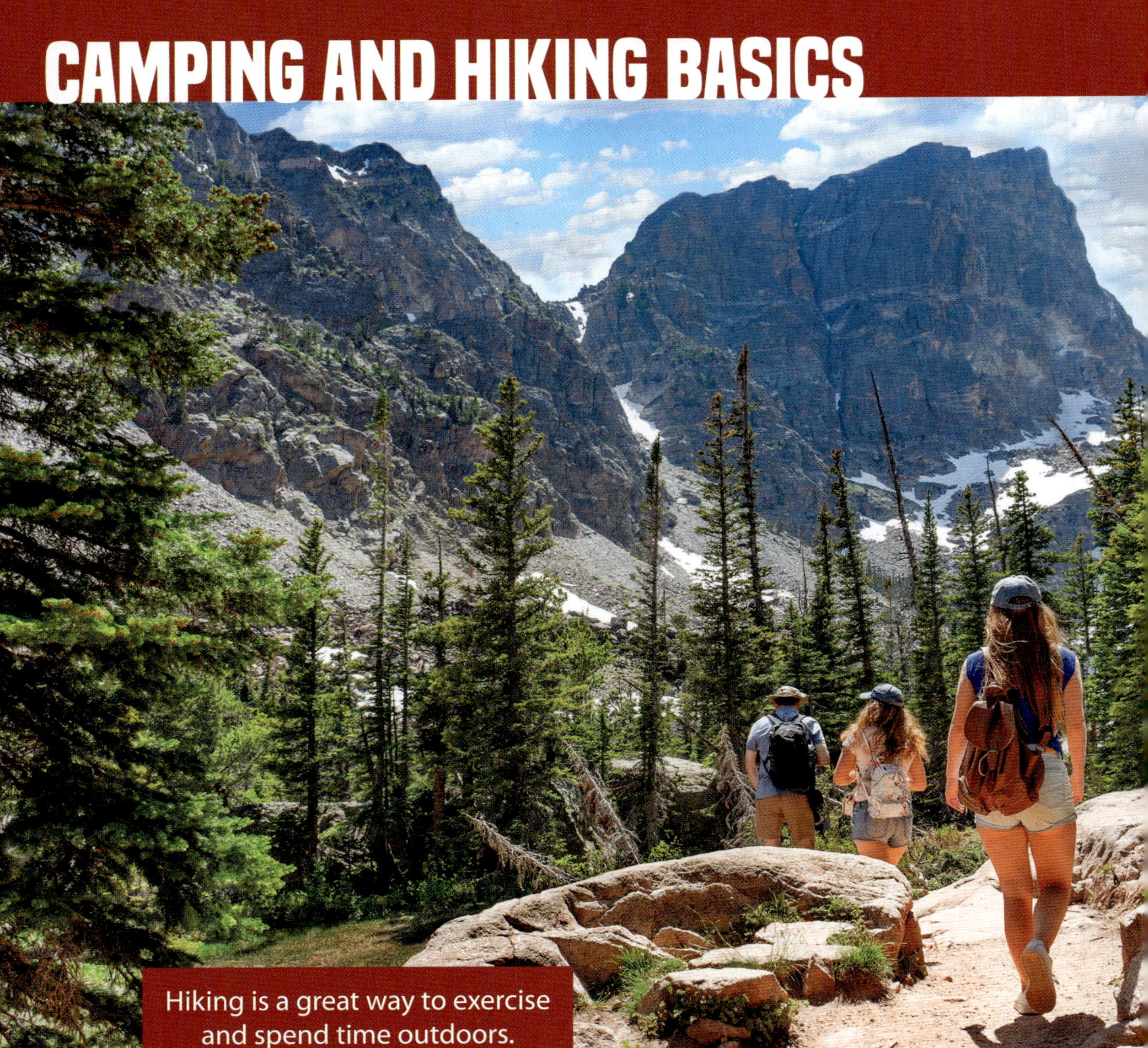

Hiking is a great way to exercise and spend time outdoors.

Many people feel drawn to wild places. Hiking and camping are popular outdoor activities. Hikers typically follow a trail through a natural area such as a forest. Camping means

spending the night away from home, typically in a tent. But camping can also mean sleeping out under the stars, in a simple shelter, or in a recreational vehicle (RV). Camping and hiking are often combined. People may camp somewhere so they can hike nearby. Or they may go on a long hike, camping each night along the way.

People may enjoy camping because it allows them to unplug from technology.

Studies show that spending time outdoors can build self-esteem and confidence.

Some people camp or hike to challenge themselves. Outdoor adventures can test the limits of the body and mind. Hiking is great exercise that increases strength, stamina, balance, and coordination.

Camping and hiking can also be relaxing. People may find peace and happiness outdoors. Many studies have shown that spending time outdoors benefits physical and mental health. Sun exposure causes the body to

DID YOU KNOW?

The COVID-19 pandemic made camping and hiking more popular. The virus that causes COVID-19 can spread more easily indoors. Outdoor activities provided people with safer ways to spend time with friends and family.

create vitamin D, a nutrient that is essential for healthy bones. Going outside, even just to sit in a forested area, reduces stress levels. Nature also boosts mood. Spending time in green spaces or near water is shown to reduce symptoms of anxiety and depression. Getting exercise while outside increases these health benefits. Hiking encourages mindfulness, a state in which people become more present and aware of their feelings.

These activities have social benefits too. Camping and hiking are great ways to bond with friends and family. In addition, many people meet new friends on the trail or at a campground.

Camping can be a way to spend quality time with family.

THE OUTDOORS ARE FOR EVERYONE

People of almost any age and ability can enjoy camping and hiking. Short hikes typically do not require special skills or expensive equipment. Camping can be more costly, especially when preparing for a first trip. However, people usually have to buy camping equipment only once. They will have the gear they need for the next trip, and camping will cost much less. For that reason, camping tends to be less expensive than other vacations.

A new tent and other gear can be expensive purchases for campers.

People who do not spend much time outdoors or are not very active may be nervous to start camping or hiking. But they can still enjoy these activities. Some campgrounds have showers and shops that may be helpful for beginning campers. People can also camp in RVs instead of tents. Short day hikes are a good starting point for new hikers.

While many people enjoy camping and hiking, these activities can be challenging. Hiking often requires dealing

People can research trails online to see if they match their ability levels.

with obstacles such as hills, rocks, roots, and mud. It can be difficult for someone with mobility issues to move on uneven ground. However, many campgrounds and trails are becoming more accessible to wheelchairs and strollers. Disabled Hikers is an organization that shares information about campsites and hiking trails. It helps people with disabilities access and enjoy the outdoors.

GETTING STARTED

To stay safe, hikers and campers need to prepare for the area they plan to visit. They should plan for the weather and the terrain. They should make sure to pack all the equipment they need, including water, food, shelter, and other gear. Hikers and campers must know how to take care of their daily needs outdoors—possibly away from modern conveniences such as toilets and electricity.

Once people arrive at a hiking trail or camping spot, they should strive to "leave no trace." This common phrase encourages respect for nature and for other people who are hiking and camping. Everyone deserves to experience the outdoors. While hiking and camping, people should explore, enjoy, and protect nature.

Campers and hikers should make sure they have all the gear they need before heading outdoors.

ESSENTIAL GEAR

It is important to spend time carefully planning what gear to bring and packing it. Many hiking trails and camping spots are located far from shops, so it is difficult to buy a quick replacement for forgotten gear. However, it is also important not to overpack on camping and hiking trips. Carrying unnecessary gear can be uncomfortable and tiring.

Having all the gear one needs can make a hiking or camping trip safer and more enjoyable.

Food and water are important gear to bring on hikes. Camping requires additional equipment such as shelter and cooking supplies. Boots, tents, backpacks, and other essentials can be quite expensive, but they tend to last a very long time. For a first trip, it may be possible to borrow gear from a friend or family member or buy used items. Different types of camping and hiking adventures require different gear. However, some equipment is essential for any trip into the outdoors.

BACKPACKS

Hikers carry their gear in backpacks or packs. For short day hikes, a small pack may have enough space to carry the gear a hiker needs. Longer expeditions require more gear. A larger backpack is necessary for these hikes.

Backpacks should be worn over both shoulders. They should fit snugly against the back and be comfortable to wear. Wide, padded shoulder straps can reduce stress on the shoulders. Hikers and campers should not wear backpacks that are too heavy for them. Wearing a backpack incorrectly or one that is too heavy can cause back, shoulder, and neck pain. This pain can become chronic. For long, challenging hikes, a backpack with a waist belt is recommended. This helps keep the backpack in place. If a backpack moves around, it could cause a person to lose his or her balance and fall.

A waist belt also causes most of a pack's weight to rest on the hips. This relieves strain on the shoulders and back. Some backpacks are built with a sturdy frame that also reduces

strain on the body. The frame is on the outside of traditional packs. But many modern packs have an internal frame. These frames can help people carry more weight and additional gear.

Some backpacks have other features in addition to waist belts and frames. These features can be helpful for longer hikes. For example, packs with mesh paneling on the back allow air to flow and reduce sweating. Some packs come with plastic bags that hold water. These bags are called hydration reservoirs. The reservoir has a long hose that acts as a straw. This pack feature allows hikers to drink water without having to stop and remove a water bottle from the pack.

Hydration reservoirs come in different sizes. Larger reservoirs are more suitable for longer or more strenuous activities.

Packing smartly can help save time and energy on a camping or hiking trip. Items that do not need to be used often should go at the bottom of the pack. The heaviest items should go in the middle, close to the straps. This keeps the majority of the pack's weight close to the hiker's body, making it easier to carry. Lighter items such as sleeping pads or bags should be packed farther from the straps or even hang from the outside of the pack. Trekking poles are another optional

DID YOU KNOW?

Some backpacks have a tiny whistle built into the buckle of the chest strap. This whistle can be blown during an emergency. It lets others know that someone needs help.

accessory that many hikers use. They help a person balance on slippery or steep trails. These can be attached to the outside of most packs. Items that will be needed during the day should go at the top of the pack.

Hikers and campers should protect their packs from the weather. If rain is forecast, hikers need a way to keep their packs and gear dry. They can put a plastic garbage bag or other liner into the pack before loading it. Small plastic bags can help protect phones or other electronic devices. A large rain poncho will often fit over both a hiker and his or her pack. A hiker can also use a waterproof cover designed to fit over a pack.

Having a waterproof pack and waterproof clothing is important when spending time outdoors.

FOOD

Hikers may not need to bring much food for a hike that is a few hours or less. But snacks can provide a boost of energy if the hike is more challenging than expected. More food is necessary for longer hikes and camping. These activities can be tiring. Healthy foods that are full of nutrients can restore energy. Since hikers will not have access to a refrigerator, it is important to bring food and snacks that will not spoil. Campers may have a cooler to prevent food from spoiling. People should also pack food, water, treats, and a water dish if they are traveling with a pet.

Snacks can boost a hiker's mood in challenging conditions.

Healthy trail snacks include granola bars, dried fruits and vegetables, nuts or seeds, and shelf-stable chicken or beef jerky. In addition to being full of nutrients, these snacks are also easy to carry. Some people prepare trail mix to take on hikes. Trail mix may contain any combination of nuts, seeds, dried fruit, granola, and chocolate candy. Some people refer to trail mix as gorp. Fresh fruits, such as bananas, apples, or oranges, are also nutritious snacks.

Other foods are not good options for hiking. Snacks like potato chips and candy bars are high in fats and sugar. They can be hard for the body to digest. While sugar can provide a quick boost of energy, the energy will not last long. High levels of salt and sugar also cause the body to use water more quickly. People can become dehydrated if they eat too much of these foods without drinking water. They may begin to feel weak or lightheaded. In addition, some foods do not make good trail snacks because they are bulky and difficult to pack. For example, chips are not a good hiking snack. Though chips are lightweight, a chip bag takes up a lot of space in a pack.

When people are hiking, they use a lot of energy. The body burns carbohydrates for energy. Carbohydrates include sugar, bread, pasta, and potatoes. Eating these foods can help hikers recover from a long hike. Carbohydrates can also help people prepare for a hike. A breakfast that is high in nutrients and calories is helpful. A breakfast burrito or oatmeal with dried fruit can give people the energy they need to start their day on the trails. Because their bodies are using energy quickly, hikers should have a light snack every hour. This gives them the energy to continue the hike.

Eating foods rich in carbohydrates, such as breads and pasta, in the days leading up to a hike can provide the body with energy.

Campers should know how to safely use cooking equipment.

People also lose electrolytes as they hike or exercise. Electrolytes include sodium, potassium, magnesium, and calcium. They are lost through sweat. The body needs electrolytes to function properly. Sports drinks can be a source of electrolytes. They also help hikers stay hydrated. Some stores sell energy gels or chews that are high in electrolytes. Lightly salted snacks, such as pretzels and nuts, also restore electrolyte levels. Eating these foods is especially important in hot weather, when people sweat more.

Electrolytes are necessary for the body to use water and nutrients.

Hot dogs are a good food option for campers because they are easy to prepare.

Campers also need to think about the food they pack. They will not have the appliances they have in their kitchens at home. Hiking trail snacks are also a good option for campers. These foods do not need much preparation. Peanut butter sandwiches are easy to make and have many calories.

Foods like rice and pasta can be cooked over a campfire or camp stove. Soup can be heated over a fire as well.

If people are camping for several days, they need to pack foods that do not spoil easily. Canned fruits and vegetables are good sources of nutrients. The sealed cans help preserve

Soups can be prepared ahead of a camping trip and heated up for meals.

the food. Campers can also take a cooler with them. This can expand the types of foods they are able to bring. For example, eggs have a lot of protein. But they need to be stored at temperatures below 68 degrees Fahrenheit (20°C) to keep from spoiling. Coolers also give campers the option to bring meat, milk, yogurt, and other perishable foods. These foods should be eaten at the beginning of a trip.

Roasting marshmallows is a popular camping activity.

MORE S'MORES, PLEASE!

S'mores are a popular camping dessert. They have three ingredients: marshmallows, chocolate, and graham crackers. Campers roast a marshmallow over a fire until it is gooey. Next, they put the hot marshmallow on top of a graham cracker along with a piece of chocolate. Another graham cracker goes on top so that the s'more looks like a sandwich. The recipe for s'mores was first published in a Girl Scout manual in 1927. The name at the time was "some more." This eventually got shortened to "s'more."

Campers should also consider the weather when packing food. They might take less perishable food during the summer, because the hot weather may cause food to spoil more quickly. If camping during the fall or winter, tea, coffee, and hot chocolate can be nice drinks that keep campers warm. People should avoid packing eggs and fresh vegetables in cold temperatures. These foods can freeze. Dry foods like pasta, granola, and dried fruits are better options.

A thermos helps maintain the temperature of liquids. It prevents heat from entering or escaping.

WATER

It is important to stay hydrated when camping and hiking.
People should drink water regularly when exercising, even if
they do not feel thirsty. An adult needs about 0.5 quarts (0.5 L)
of water for every hour of hiking. Children need less. Both
adults and children may need to drink more than this amount
if the weather is hot or the hike is challenging. Hiking at high
altitudes may also require drinking more water.

Symptoms of dehydration include a headache and feeling tired.

If people do not drink enough water, they can become dehydrated. This occurs more often during intense exercise and in hot weather. Dehydration can be serious. It can cause people to become extremely thirsty and tired. They may experience dizziness or confusion. Dehydration can also lead to dangerous and potentially deadly conditions, such as heatstroke. Severe dehydration requires medical attention.

Drinking water protects against dehydration. It is more helpful to take regular sips of water than to drink a lot all at once. People can prepare their bodies for long hikes by drinking water before hitting the trails. In addition to drinking enough water, people need to make sure they have enough electrolytes. Electrolytes help balance water levels in the body.

Drinking water regularly before, during, and after a hike reduces the risk of dehydration.

Hikers and campers should always bring water or containers to fill with water. Campsites usually have clean drinking water available, but most hiking trails do not. Before leaving on a trip, campers and hikers should research water availability. They should bring all the water they need. Hikers should not be afraid to bring more water than seems necessary. It is better to have too much water than to not have enough.

A person can typically survive for several weeks without any food. But they can survive for only a few days without water.

Hikers and campers should not drink water directly from natural sources, as they could contain harmful bacteria.

Dressing in layers is a good way to prepare for changes in weather.

CLOTHING AND SHOES

Hikers and campers should check the weather forecast before packing clothes for their destinations. Being too hot or too cold can make a trip outdoors less enjoyable. It can also be dangerous to a person's health.

It is important to keep in mind that weather forecasts are not always accurate. Altitude can also affect the weather and temperature. Hikers and campers should be prepared for changes in weather. Packing layers, such as a T-shirt, sweatshirt, and rain jacket, is recommended. Layered clothing makes it easier to adjust to changes in weather. Hikers and campers should have a comfortable inner layer, a warm middle layer, and a waterproof outer layer. The legs of some hiking pants zip off so that they can be worn as either long pants or shorts.

Clothing material is also important to consider. Lightweight clothing is less tiring to carry. Clothing should also be warm and dry quickly. Some hikers prefer nylon because of these qualities. Cotton is not recommended. Though it is light, the material does not help people keep warm or stay cool. It also takes a long time to dry. This can be an issue if it rains or after working up a sweat from a hike. Wet clothing draws heat away from the body. This is also why waterproof rain gear such as a jacket or poncho is necessary when spending several days outdoors.

Gaiters can be worn over shoes. These waterproof covers prevent water, rocks, and other materials from getting inside shoes.

In addition to standard clothing, several additional items can help protect against the weather. People should wear sunscreen whenever they spend time outdoors. It protects against the sun's ultraviolet (UV) rays that cause sunburns and some forms of skin cancer. Sunglasses and a hat with a brim add further protection from the sun. Some people drape wet bandannas around their necks to help them keep cool.

Warm gloves and socks are necessary when spending time outdoors in cold weather. The hands and feet tend to get cold more quickly than other parts of the body.

Preparing for cold weather is just as important. People should pack layers of warm clothing, including a scarf, mittens, coat, hiking socks, and an extra change of dry clothes. A hat is extremely important. People lose a lot of warmth through their heads.

Campers and hikers must also think about their footwear. Sneakers offer enough support and protection during short hikes. But for long treks, comfortable hiking boots are essential. A good pair of hiking boots reduces the risk of falls. Trekking poles can provide additional stability.

It is important to try on new boots and break them in before a long trip. Some hikers and backpackers also wear special hiking socks. They may put sock liners under their socks. This combination helps keep feet dry and prevent blisters. For camping trips that do not require much hiking, a supportive pair of shoes may not be necessary. Campers do not need to wear shoes when they are in a tent or cabin. But they should wear them outside. Because of this, slip-on shoes or sandals are a good choice because they can be put on and taken off easily.

Campers and hikers may make the mistake of packing too much clothing. This can add extra weight to a person's pack. Clothes can also take up a lot of space. Some backpackers recommend bringing only two outfits: one for hiking and one for sleeping. There are ways to fold clothes so that they take up less space in a pack. Clothing should first be folded in half. Then it should be rolled tightly.

Breaking in hiking boots helps prevent blisters on a long hike.

Setting up a tent can be challenging, so it is recommended that people practice before a trip.

SHELTER AND BEDDING

For tenting camping trips or hikes that last several days, people will need to pack shelter. This includes a tent and sleeping bag. There are many types of tents and sleeping bags. People should consider the climate of the destination when choosing their equipment. Additional gear, such as an extra blanket or rain tarp, can also be packed to make camping safer and more enjoyable.

Many people camp in tents. A tent serves as a temporary shelter. It protects a person from rain, wind, wildlife, and insects. When purchasing a tent, people should consider the tent's size. Tents are measured by their sleeping capacity. For example, the floor of a four-person tent can fit four unrolled sleeping bags. If four people sleep in a four-person tent, there will be little room for other gear. People often choose tents with a larger sleeping capacity than the number of people going on the trip. For example, a group of four people may choose to camp in a six-person tent. This gives them more space.

Most tents are made from waterproof materials, such as nylon and polyester.

It is important to stake down tent corners, especially in windy weather. This keeps the tent in place.

People should think about the size and weight of a tent before making a purchase. A heavy and bulky tent is difficult to carry on trails. Backpackers may need to hike far distances before setting up camp. They may choose to follow the sleeping capacity so they are not carrying extra weight.

Weather conditions also determine what tent is best for a trip. Summer tents are best for hot weather. They are built to have good airflow but are not designed to withstand harsh weather conditions. A three-season or four-season tent is a better fit for people who want to camp throughout the year.

Three-season tents can be used in the spring, summer, and fall. They are built to withstand heavy wind and rain. Four-season tents are even more durable. They are necessary for people camping in cold weather and snowy conditions.

All campers should practice setting up their tents before going on a trip. This preparation makes it easier to set up the tent at the campsite. It also is a way to check that no pieces of the tent are missing. Campers need to prepare for moisture and rainfall. A ground cover, which is also called a footprint, goes underneath the tent. The campsite may be wet. The ground cover protects the floor of the tent from moisture. It also protects the tent from rocks, sticks, or other objects that could damage it. A rain cover or tarp can be put over the tent. These items are sometimes called rainflys. They block rain from getting into the tent and keep gear dry.

Backpackers may camp in minimalist structures that are more lightweight than other tents.

Sleeping bags are also important gear. It can get cold in a tent at night, even during the summer. A warm, comfortable sleeping bag is necessary. The temperature rating of a sleeping bag indicates the lowest temperature the bag should be used in. The fit of a sleeping bag also matters. Rectangular bags are loose fitting and give the camper more space to move around. Backpackers may prefer a close-fitting sleeping bag. Semirectangular bags and mummy bags are close fitting to trap body heat.

The outer part of a sleeping bag is called the shell. It comes in many materials, such as polyester and nylon. These materials are waterproof. The insulation, or fill, may be down or synthetic. Down is usually lighter and warmer than synthetic fill. However, synthetic insulation tends to be cheaper and dries faster if it gets wet.

BACKPACKING SHELTERS

People may want to carry as little weight as possible when backpacking. They may choose to use a minimalist shelter rather than a tent. For instance, a tarp shelter is a single tarp mounted on poles. It does not have a floor. It protects backpackers from rain and snow. Some people may sleep in hammock tents, which are hammocks with rain tarps that cover them. Bivvy sacks are barriers that that go around sleeping bags. They can be zipped up all the way. They are made of special fabric that allows the person to breathe while inside.

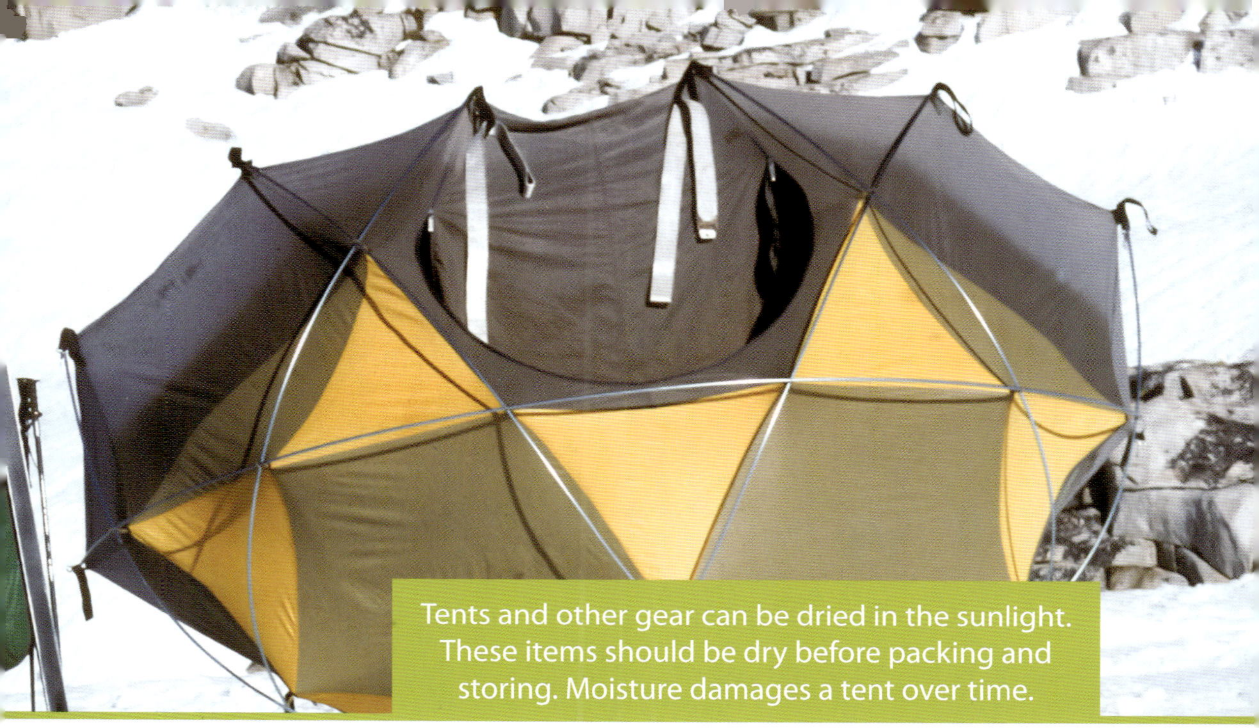

Tents and other gear can be dried in the sunlight. These items should be dry before packing and storing. Moisture damages a tent over time.

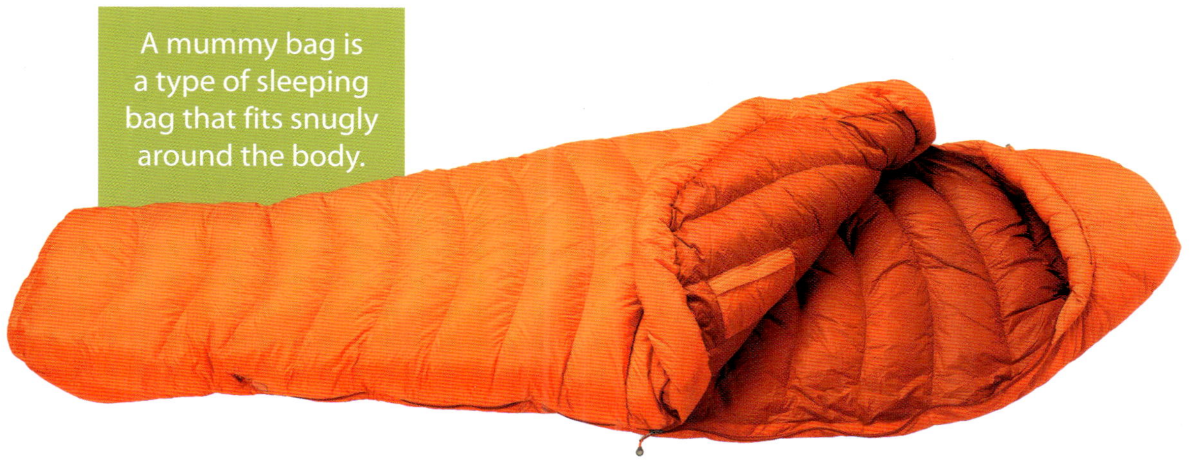

Sleeping bags can be stored in stuff sacks to make packing up and hiking easier. But sleeping bags should not be stored in stuff sacks when not traveling. Sleeping bags need to air out to stay dry and clean. This also prevents the fill from becoming compressed. Fill becomes less insulating if it is packed down.

A mummy bag is a type of sleeping bag that fits snugly around the body.

It may be convenient to roll sleeping bags for travel. However, sleeping bags should not be rolled during long-term storage as this can damage the gear.

People who are camping close to their cars have the option of taking other bedding materials. A sleeping pad is like a portable mattress. Some are inflatable. Others are made of foam. People may also choose to bring an air mattress, camping cot, or camping pillow. These items can make sleeping in a tent more comfortable. But they also weigh a lot or take up space. For these reasons, some people prefer not to use these items when backpacking.

DID YOU KNOW?

Most backpackers do not bring a pillow. A rolled-up sweatshirt or towel packed into a stuff sack can function as a pillow.

An inflatable mattress
pad can make
sleeping outdoors
more comfortable.

Always have water nearby before starting a campfire.

COOKING EQUIPMENT

Campers must also pack gear to prepare food for meals. They should research whether the campsite allows fires. If so, campers should know how to safely start and extinguish a fire.

They will need firewood and fire starters, such as matches. Fire starters should be kept in a waterproof container. People should also have water nearby to put out the flames.

Campers may bring camp stoves with them. These appliances are portable and come in many shapes and sizes. They need fuel such as propane or butane. A windscreen prevents the flame from blowing out.

Camp stoves are better for the environment than campfires because they produce less smoke.

In addition to fire starters, fuel, and a camp stove, campers need to pack pots, pans, and utensils. They also need to bring the tools required to cook each meal. If canned foods are on the menu, they will need a can opener. If they are going to make pancakes, they need a spatula. Other items to consider include dishes, tongs, oven mitts, a tablecloth, wash basins, cooking oil, salt and pepper, and spices. Camping supply stores often offer cooking kits that include lightweight pots, cups, and other items that stack inside each other for easy packing.

Campers should plan their meals before a trip so they know what utensils to pack with them.

EMERGENCY GEAR

Hikers and campers should have emergency supplies with them in case something goes wrong. One of the most important items is a first aid kit. A basic first aid kit contains gloves, antiseptic wipes, bandages, gauze, adhesive cloth tape, and antibiotic ointment. It also contains sprays and creams to treat minor burns. Other ointments can make bug bites or rashes less itchy. Tweezers help remove splinters. Wrappings and splints provide support for sprains. Medicines to treat colds, headaches, fevers, and allergies

A basic first aid kit includes medical equipment that can be used to treat common injuries while hiking and camping.

should also be kept in a first aid kit. Hikers and campers should always bring other medications they may need, such as prescription medicines, inhalers, or injections to treat severe allergic reactions.

Some first aid kits include an emergency blanket. A person's body temperature may drop after he or she stops exercising.

This can be dangerous. The emergency blanket helps someone stay warm. If hikers and campers do not have an emergency blanket, they can use a large trash bag instead.

Other essentials include a map, a flashlight, sunscreen, and bug spray. A knife or multi-tool can be helpful in emergencies. People should be prepared with extra food, water, and warm clothing. Rope and bungee cords can be used to tie up gear, secure a temporary shelter or rain cover, or hang things up to dry. Plastic trash bags and resealable plastic bags can also be used to keep gear dry. For some trips, hikers and campers will need to bring special items. For example, bear spray is important when traveling where bear attacks are possible.

Sometimes, hiking and camping equipment will break. A multi-tool with a screwdriver and pliers can come in handy in these situations. Hikers and campers can also pack a small sewing kit and duct tape for repairs. Duct tape works especially well to temporarily repair tears or punctures in

Flashlights help hikers and campers navigate in the dark. They can also be used to signal for help.

FLASHLIGHTS

Flashlights and headlamps are important gear for camping and hiking. They help people navigate around campsites and trails when it is dark. Flashlights can also be used to signal an emergency. Flashing the light quickly three times, followed by three long flashes, and then flashing the light quickly three more times spells out SOS in Morse code. It alerts others nearby that someone needs help. When purchasing a flashlight, people should make sure that the light is bright. They should also check that the battery can last a long time. Campers may want to pack extra batteries as a backup.

tents or clothing. When campers bring inflatable pads or pillows, they may want to have repair kits on hand in case of a leak. They can also bring repair kits made for their brand of camp stove.

Wearing a headlamp is a hands-free option for hikers who are exploring at night.

Serious injuries or accidents can occur when hiking and camping. Hikers and campers need a way to call for help if they are in danger and cannot get to safety on their own. One way to contact help is on a cell phone. In places where a cell signal is not available, a whistle, a bright flashlight, or an emergency signal flare can alert others that someone needs help.

ADDITIONAL SUPPLIES

Additional gear is needed for campers and hikers who are spending several days outdoors. They will need to pack hygiene products, such as a toothbrush and toothpaste, a hairbrush, and biodegradable soap. Other items should be left at home. Some shampoos have chemicals that are bad for the environment. The scent of deodorant can attract insects and other wildlife. Some campsites have showers and public toilets. When camping in an area without a restroom, people need to bring toilet paper. They also should bring a small shovel to use for burying solid waste.

Some campsites do not have restrooms. Campers will need to bring their own toilet paper and know how to relieve themselves in nature.

Smartphones can be useful when camping and hiking. Most have built-in flashlights and cameras. In places with cell service, phones can be used to call for help. Weather apps on

In remote locations without cell reception, a satellite phone can be used to call for help in an emergency.

Fishing is a popular activity during camping trips.

phones allow people to check the weather and prepare for it. Cell phones and other electronic devices should be powered off when they are not being used to save their batteries' charge. Other forms of entertainment may be brought on some camping trips. People can unwind by playing card games or reading books. Fishing, kayaking, canoeing, and biking are other ways to enjoy the outdoors while camping.

Nearly four million households in North America went camping for the first time in 2020.

Campgrounds are the most popular camping sites. These places have designated, numbered spots for each group of campers to set up a campsite. Camping is also allowed in some rural and wilderness areas. When people camp in these areas, it is called backcountry or dispersed camping. Camping is growing in popularity. In 2021, 93.8 million North American households identified themselves as campers.

RV CAMPING AND GLAMPING

Camping does not always mean leaving behind the comforts of home. RV camping is one way to experience the outdoors in comfort. RVs offer many benefits. When camping in an RV, there is no need to pitch a tent, cook outside, or use a campground bathroom. Many RVs contain a toilet and shower. They have a kitchen that typically includes a small stove, refrigerator, and sink. Some RVs have a microwave or oven. RVs also have heating and air conditioning, which allow campers to stay comfortable in any weather.

RVs allow campers access to amenities that may not be available during other forms of camping.

RVs come in many shapes and sizes. Some are like large vans, while others are meant to be towed behind a vehicle. A small RV may be built to sleep two people. A luxury RV may fit as many as 12 people.

However, camping in an RV has limitations. Renting or purchasing an RV is expensive. Fueling such a large vehicle is also costly. In addition, people must find campsites that contain hookups for water, sewer, and electricity. They must rent a spot to camp for the night. These sites are a bit more expensive than tent sites.

Glamping is another option for campers who are prepared to spend money to be close to nature. Guests at luxury campgrounds can rent a tent or cabin. Some campgrounds offer unique shelters such as yurts, igloos, treehouses, or even old helicopters. Guests typically do not have to cook or

CAMPING CLOSE TO HOME

People do not need to travel far to go camping. People can camp in their backyards. State and regional parks also often have campgrounds. These locations can be great opportunities to try camping for the first time or test out new equipment. After getting used to camping close to home, people can go on camping trips that are farther away.

RV campgrounds may be crowded, so it is important to book a campsite ahead of time.

clean up. They usually have access to a bed and bathroom. The site may also have electricity, internet access, and other conveniences. Luxury campgrounds are similar to a stay in a hotel. However, their locations make it easier to access the outdoors and enjoy outdoor activities.

DID YOU KNOW?

The term *glamping* was first used in 2007. It is a combination of the words *glamorous* and *camping*.

CAR CAMPING

Most campers in the United States and Canada prefer to stay in tents. Car camping is one way for campers to sleep under the stars. This type of camping involves driving a car or truck to a campground or other camping location. As with RV camping, campers must rent a camping spot for the night. However, the spot is not as expensive as an area for an RV. After parking in the designated spot, campers pitch a tent nearby. People typically need to reserve a camping spot in advance. Pets are allowed at many campgrounds.

The most basic car campsite offers a single parking spot, a flat spot or platform for a tent, and a firepit or grill. Many campsites also have a picnic table. Typically, several campsites will share a bathroom and a spigot for clean water. Trash cans or a dumpster will be available as well. At some campgrounds, visitors have access to a wide range of services such as boat rentals, a swimming pool, a playground, miniature golf, an arcade, a laundry facility, or a camp store. But these campgrounds can be more costly.

Car camping allows campers to bring gear without having to carry it long distances.

BACKCOUNTRY AND DISPERSED CAMPING

More experienced campers enjoy backcountry and dispersed camping. These forms of camping occur outside of a campground. Backcountry campers may hike, canoe, kayak, bike, climb, or even ride a horse to get to a campsite. Dispersed campers do not need to travel far from their cars to camp. But they will be camping in designated

Dispersed camping occurs at least 1 mile (1.6 km) away from designated campgrounds.

A member of the US Forest Service takes apart an illegal campfire ring at a dispersed camping site. Campfires are not allowed in some dispersed and backcountry hiking sites.

wilderness areas with few amenities. Unlike car camping, dispersed camping has limited access to bathrooms, clean water, electricity, firepits, or trash disposal.

Backcountry and dispersed camping are allowed on most public lands in the United States. However, campers may need to get a permit first. They should always check the rules for camping in a specific area before setting out. For example, setting fires is not allowed in some areas.

TYPES OF HIKING

There are more than 200,000 miles (321,870 km) of public footpaths in the United States. Many trails wind through forests, but hiking paths can be found in all types of environments, such as beaches, deserts, marshes, and mountains. There are even hiking trails in cities. For example, the High Line trail in New York City is a short walk along an old elevated railway line that has been converted into a park. Some urban hiking trails are interpretive trails. These are like outdoor museums. They are typically short and accessible. They often include signs with information on the local history or nature. Other trails may feature sculptures, landmarks, historical sites, or other things to see and experience along the way.

Hiking trails have varying degrees of difficulty. Trails for beginners are typically less than 3 miles (4.8 km) long. They may be relatively flat with little gain in elevation. Some trails are paved or have boardwalks that are accessible to bikes, wheelchairs, and strollers. Challenging hikes are longer. There may be steep uphill sections and difficult terrain. Any hiking trail may have obstacles such as rocks, roots, small streams, loose gravel, mud, and steep slopes. Hikers should research a trail to decide if it is appropriate for their levels of skill and experience.

Challenging hikes may require people to wade through water.

The beginning of a hiking trail is called the trailhead. Typically, hikers can park near the trailhead. If the trailhead is in a public park or campground, there may be bathrooms, water fountains, or other services nearby. It is almost always free to hike on a trail, though there may be a parking fee. Government agencies, such as the National Park Service, build and maintain most of the trails in the United States. Nonprofit groups, such as the National Audubon Society, and local community groups also develop trails.

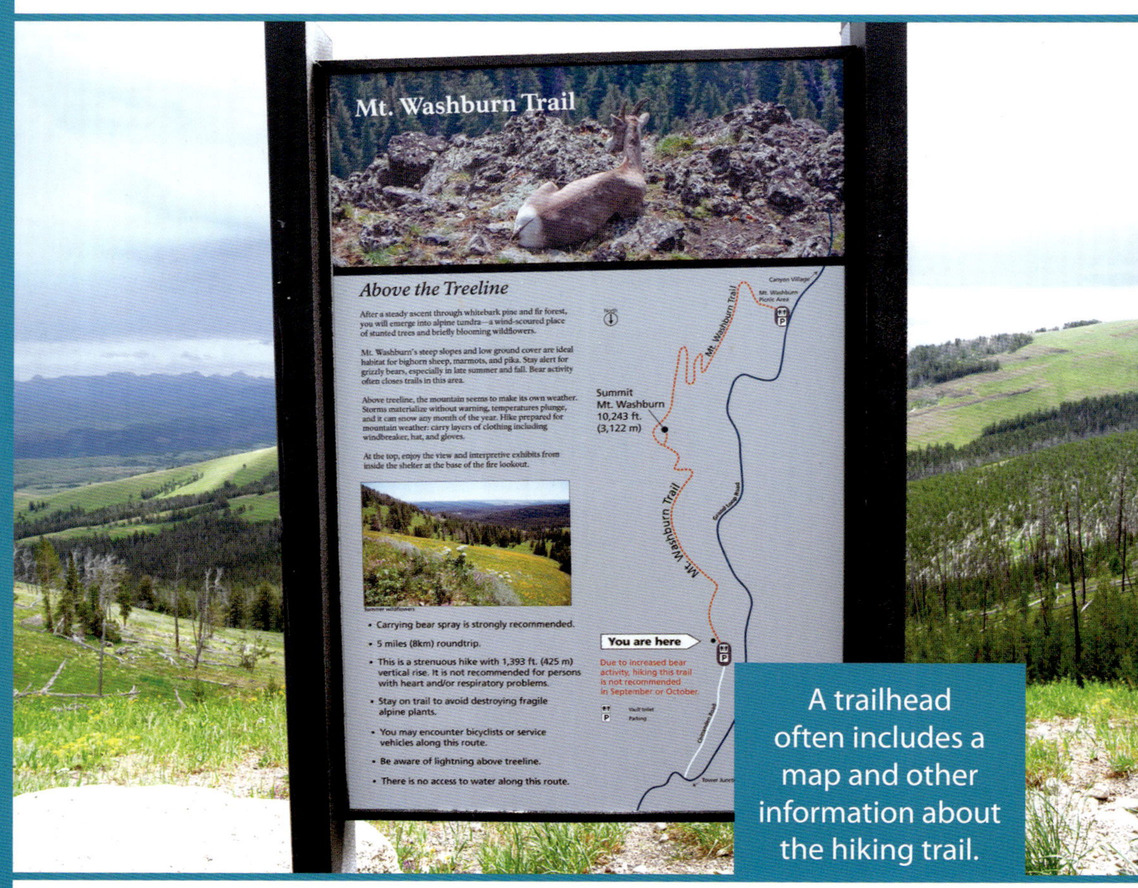

A trailhead often includes a map and other information about the hiking trail.

Trails are marked with blazes that help prevent hikers from getting lost. Blazes include wooden signs or paint smears and metal plates on trees. They are placed along the trail to show where the path is. Some trails are marked with cairns, or rocks that are stacked on top of each other. Blazes and cairns are placed so that they are easily visible to a standing adult.

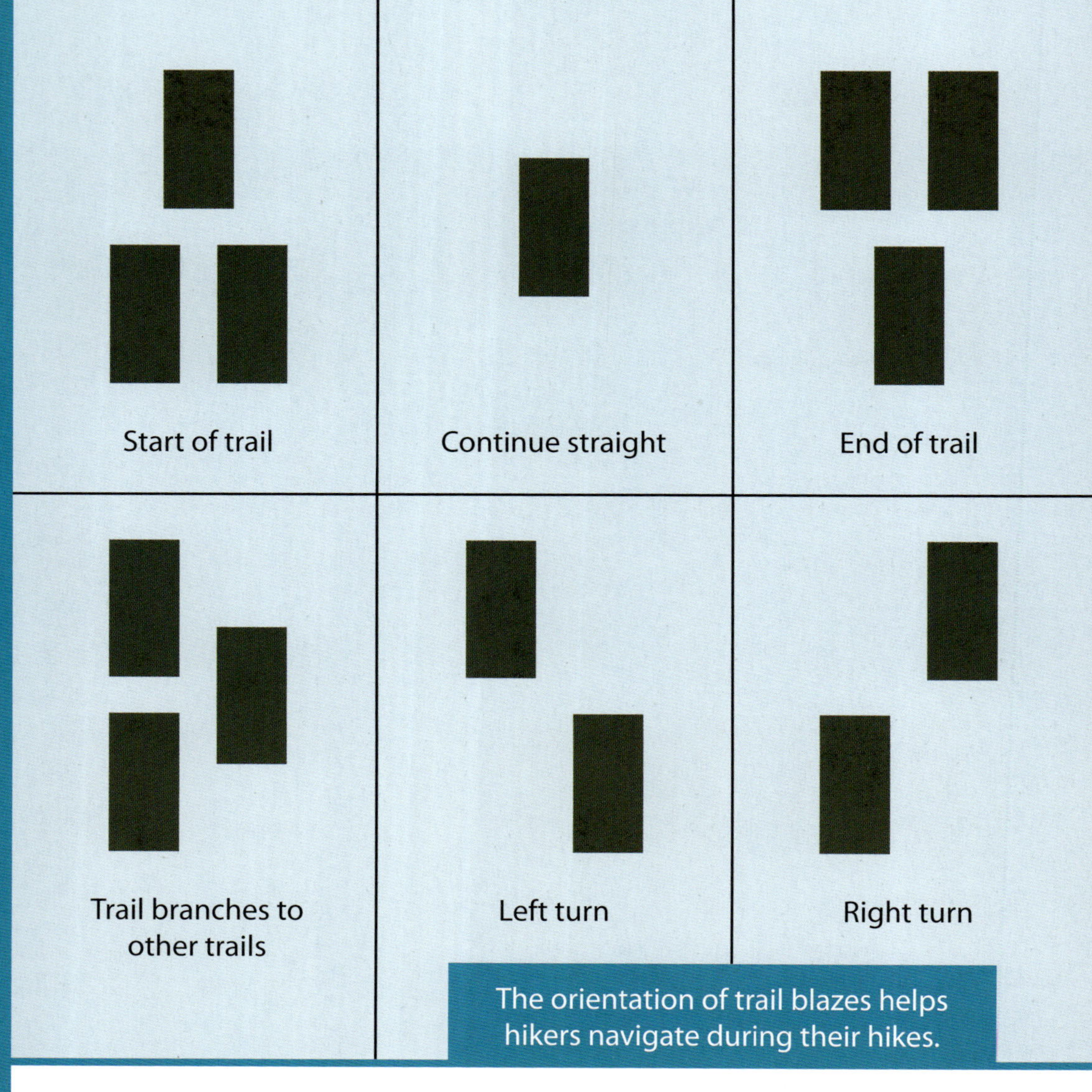

The orientation of trail blazes helps hikers navigate during their hikes.

Some hiking areas have multiple trails. Each trail will have differently colored blazes. Hikers should make sure to follow the correct color to get to their destinations. The arrangement of blazes is also important. For example, a single rectangular paint smear means the trail continues straight forward. Two paint smears mean the trail turns. Three paint smears indicate the beginning or end of a trail or a new trail branch.

DAY HIKES

Day hikes are hikes that can be completed in a single day. They range from short walks that last a couple of hours to intense adventures that may take the full day to complete. A short day hike is an easy way to enjoy time outside. People do not need to take much gear for a short hike. They may need only proper clothing and a water bottle. Longer hikes or hikes through difficult terrain will require more gear and preparation. State and regional parks often have day hiking opportunities, so people do not need to travel far from home.

Day hikes can be a good way to spend time with family.

People can search online for nearby day hikes. They should check the weather before heading out and plan accordingly. Sometimes a trail map can be found online. Printing the map or taking a screenshot on a cell phone can be helpful to navigate the trail. When selecting a trail for a day hike, a person should keep his or her athletic ability in mind. Hiking on difficult terrain or uphill is more tiring than walking on flat ground. A short day hike that does not have much elevation gain is often a good place to start for beginning hikers.

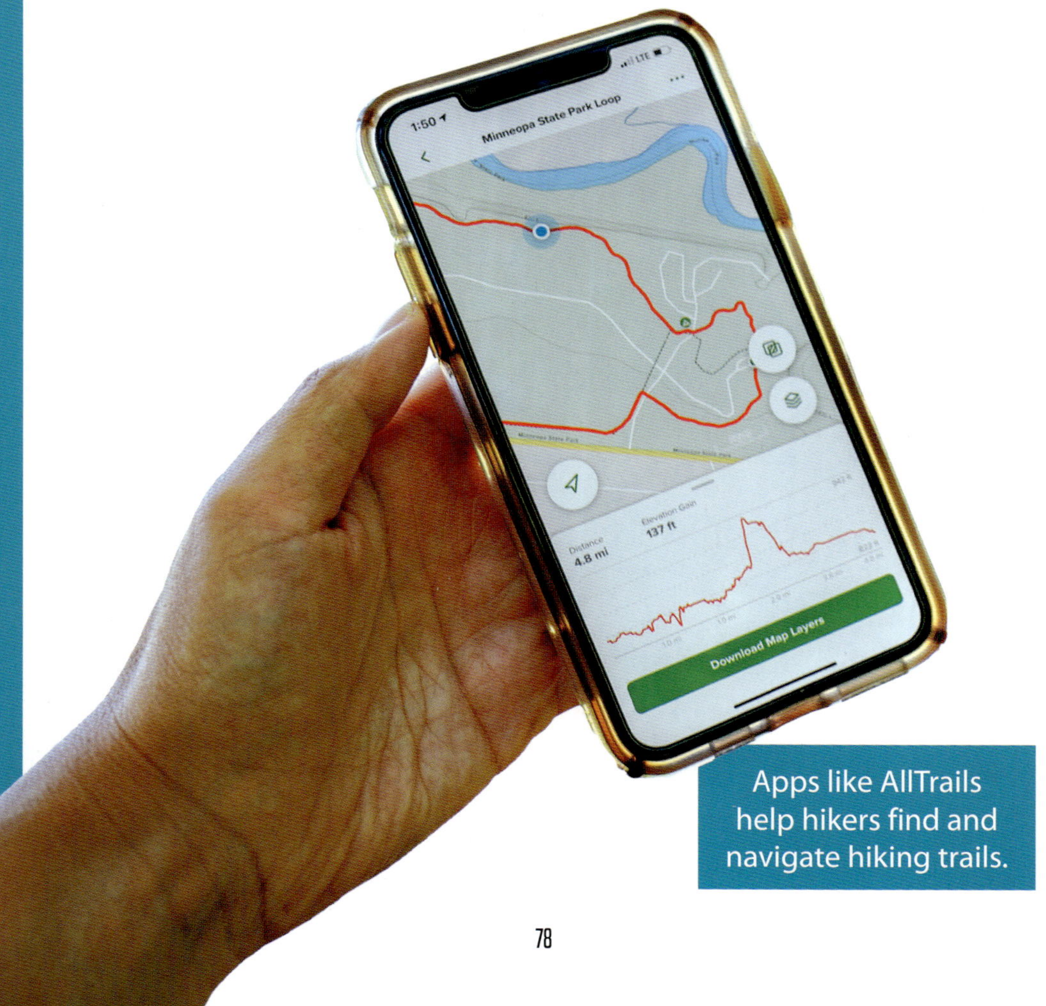

Apps like AllTrails help hikers find and navigate hiking trails.

CHALLENGING HIKES

The longer a hike is, the more challenging it will be. Trails with steep paths and high elevation gains will also test a hiker's endurance. Summit hikes and canyon hikes can be challenging, especially for beginners. Summit hikes lead to the top of a mountain. Those who enjoy hiking for scenic views will find summit hikes rewarding. These hikes offer a sweeping view of the landscape. Canyon hikes lead down into the bottom of a canyon, gorge, or ravine. Hikers need to be prepared to walk uphill for the return trip.

People may experience leg cramps while hiking. Stretching the sore area and staying hydrated can help reduce pain.

Hiking up a slope can be tiring. It requires a lot of strength from muscles in the backs of the legs, such as the calves and hamstrings. Hiking downhill uses many muscles in the fronts of the legs, including the quadriceps. Some summit hikes are easier than others. Strenuous summit trails may require hikers to scramble over steep sections of boulders, rocks, snow, or ice.

Mountain climbing is another way to reach the summit. It requires extra gear, such as rope, a helmet, a harness, and special shoes. Mountain climbing can be very challenging. People should train before scaling a mountain. Beginners should travel with a guide or an expert. Some mountain summits are not suitable for beginners. Mountain climbing can be a fulfilling experience. Climbers are rewarded with

NIGHT HIKES

Some people enjoy the challenge of hiking at night. Night hiking can be dangerous. Because it is harder to see, there is a higher risk of falling or getting lost. Night hikers should pick a trail that they have already hiked during the daytime and go on a night with a full moon. They should also bring flashlights or headlamps. Night hikes can be appealing because they allow hikers to spot nighttime wildlife. Hikers can also plan to reach a peak or viewpoint in time to watch a dazzling sunrise.

stunning views. Some people attempt to hike all of the mountains in a certain area or over a certain height. These people are known as peakbaggers.

Some experienced hikers may choose to travel in places without trails. This is called backcountry hiking. It requires a high level of preparation and advanced outdoor skills. When there is no trail, getting lost is more of a risk. However, it can be thrilling to explore an area that very few other people visit.

People use muscles throughout their
bodies while rock climbing.

Backpacking trips can offer the opportunity to camp in remote locations.

BACKPACKING

Backpacking is a combination of hiking and camping. People need to travel with a pack that holds everything they need to survive in the wilderness when backpacking. They typically hike during the day and camp out at night. Backpackers travel beyond the borders of a campground. They may spend several

days on the trail, allowing them to travel longer distances than day hikers. However, backpacking is more difficult than camping or hiking. It requires more preparation and planning. It also requires special gear. Backpackers need to carry camping and hiking supplies. Items should be small and lightweight so they can fit into a pack and be carried easily. Lightweight gear tends to be expensive. Backpacking can also be dangerous. Backpackers may be hiking and camping in remote locations. They should know how to administer first aid and how to get help in emergencies.

Some backpackers challenge themselves to thru-hiking. This means they walk the entire length of a long trail. For example, the Appalachian Trail runs for approximately 2,190 miles (3,524 km) from Georgia to Maine. It can take five to seven months to hike the entire trail. Thru-hikers must stop regularly in towns or cities along the way to replenish their supplies. They often rely on other people they meet on the trail for

M. J. Eberhart, *center*, completed his third thru-hike of the Appalachian Trail in 2021. He was 83 at the time, becoming the oldest person to thru-hike the trail.

Approximately three million people hike a part of the Appalachian Trail each year.

help and support. Thru-hikes can be stressful physically and mentally. Seventy-five percent of the people who begin a thru-hike of the Appalachian Trail do not complete it.

Backpacking trips do not need to last for months. A backpacking trip can be a day hike and a single overnight stay. Backpackers may also choose to tackle a longer trail in chunks. For example, a backpacker may spend two weeks hiking part of a trail. He or she may return later to hike more of it.

DID YOU KNOW?

A fully loaded backpacking pack typically weighs 30 to 35 pounds (14 to 16 kg).

Following the Leave No Trace guidelines helps protect natural spaces so that they can be enjoyed by others.

The natural spaces used for camping and hiking need to be protected. Campers and hikers should limit the effects they have on the environment. For example, they should make sure they do not leave trash behind. They should not take rocks, plants, or other objects as collectibles. The organization Leave No Trace has guidelines for how to respectfully enjoy the outdoors.

The organization reminds campers and hikers to plan for their trips. Thorough planning can lead to a more enjoyable experience. For example, if campers know that heavy rain is in the forecast, they can prepare by bringing rain gear and warm clothes. Planning also keeps the outdoors safe. Some campgrounds do not allow open fires during certain times of the year when weather conditions increase the risk of wildfires. Campers who have not planned ahead may not have other ways to cook their food. They may try to set a fire anyway. This is dangerous. A fire that burns out of control can be very destructive.

Heavy rain can make it impossible to cook on a campfire or camp stove. Campers should have other meals planned if rain is in the forecast.

Hikers should stay on trails as much as possible. Wandering off-trail can harm plant life. If many people wander off-trail, it is difficult for plants to recover. It can also be dangerous. Hikers may be tempted to leave the trail and look over a steep edge or cliff. They may want to climb rocks. But this can lead to falls and injuries.

Trails are maintained to keep hikers safe. When hikers wander off-trail, they are at greater risk of tripping or falling because the ground is more uneven.

Sometimes people need to go off-trail to relieve themselves. When exploring off-trail, hikers should walk on durable surfaces as much as possible. Rock, sand, and gravel are not as easily damaged as plants and soil.

Dry grasses and sedges are more durable than other plants because of their strong roots and thick stems.

Campers also need to know how to minimize their impacts on wilderness areas. At popular campsites, campers should pitch their tents in heavily trafficked areas to reduce damage to other areas of land. When backcountry camping, people should set up camp on durable surfaces. If this is not possible, they should move the tent every day, even if staying in the same area. If camping in a group with multiple tents, they should make sure tents are spaced apart. Campers should also minimize how much they walk around the area. These practices reduce damage to the land.

People need to know how to properly dispose of waste. Many campgrounds and trailheads have trash cans available. In other locations, people should be prepared to pack up their trash. When trash is not disposed of correctly, it can attract wildlife and introduce human foods into their diets. Trash should never be burned or buried. Campers and hikers also need to know how to get rid of human waste, which can run into waterways and make them unsafe to drink from.

When hiking, people are responsible for packing up trash and food scraps, such as apple cores and banana peels.

In general, campers and hikers should strive to leave outdoor spaces as they found them. They should not cut branches off trees or pick wildflowers. These actions and many others are harmful to the wilderness. Many animals rely on plants for food and shelter. People may think there is not much of an impact if they take only a few flowers. But these actions add up if everybody has the same idea. In some places, removing natural objects is illegal.

Campers and hikers can take pictures to record the plant and animal life they see during their trips.

Campers and hikers should also respect wildlife. Animals can be photographed from a distance, but people should not touch or feed wild animals. These actions are stressful to animals. They can also put people in danger. Animals can carry disease. They may attack and injure people when stressed. It is also important that people do not leave trash behind. Leftovers and trash can attract wildlife. Eating these items is unhealthy for animals, and the creatures can become dependent on humans for food. This can lead to dangerous encounters between people and wildlife.

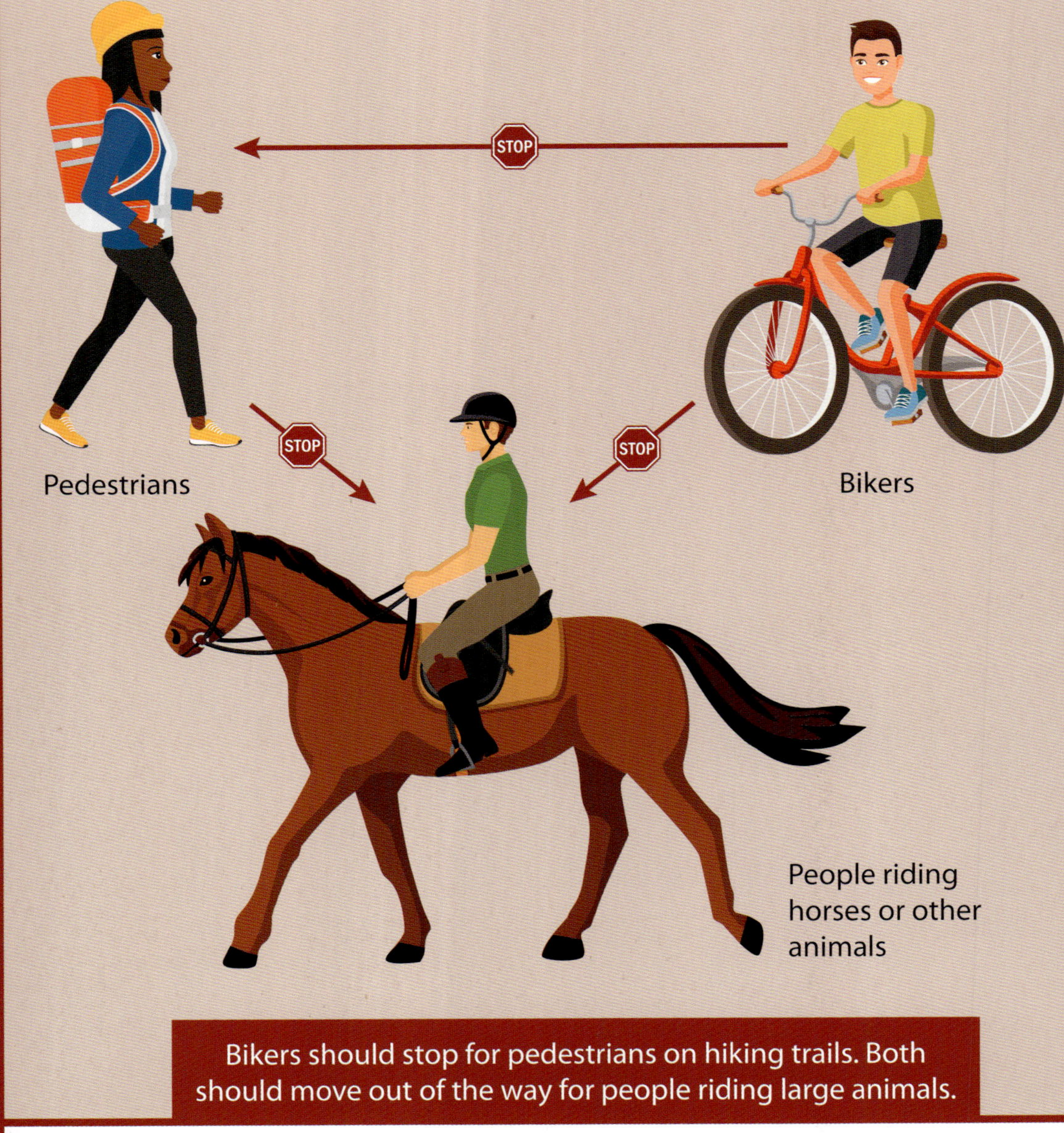

Bikers should stop for pedestrians on hiking trails. Both should move out of the way for people riding large animals.

Similarly, campers should know how to build fires to have as little impact on the outdoors as possible. Camp stoves do not require firewood and have little effect on the natural space. If campers build a campfire, they should know how to safely start and extinguish it.

People should also be respectful of others while enjoying the outdoors. The wilderness is a shared space where many people go to relax. Listening to music while hiking may be enjoyable to some, but others may prefer the sounds of nature. Hikers can use earbuds while on the trails to be considerate of others. Trail etiquette also includes stepping aside to let faster hikers pass. Certain trails and campgrounds may require pets to be leashed at all times.

On narrow paths, hikers traveling downhill should step out of the way to allow hikers traveling uphill to pass.

Following these principles helps others have more fun outdoors. It helps preserve wilderness areas so that people can enjoy them for a long time. By aiming to leave no trace, hikers and campers keep themselves and the natural world safe.

A paper map can be useful in emergencies when a cell phone or other navigational device breaks or runs out of batteries.

Trail markers along hiking paths can give information about distances to destinations.

NAVIGATION

Navigation is an important skill to have when spending time outdoors. Hikers and campers need to know where they are, where they are going, and how to get there. For some hikes, people can use their phones to navigate. Other hikes may be deeper in the wilderness, where cell service is unreliable. In those cases, people should be prepared with a paper map and a compass.

The US Geological Survey makes maps of all national trails and recreational areas. These maps are available for free online. Many other public trails also have free online maps. Paper maps may also be available at the trailhead. The trailhead typically includes a large map of the trail as well. Hikers can bring a printed map from home or use a provided paper map. They can also take a photo of the map at the trailhead to use for navigation. People should refer to the map regularly while hiking to make sure they are still on the route they planned to take. Blazes and cairns along the hiking trail also help hikers stay on the correct path.

Compass needles are magnetized. They point north because of Earth's magnetic field.

GETTING LOST

Even experienced hikers can get lost. They may find themselves off-trail. Bad weather can cause someone to get separated from the group. When lost, hikers should remember to STOP: sit, think, observe, and plan. If they can find a trail, they should stay on that trail. If not, they should try to contact help, stay in one place, and wait for rescue.

People can put their navigational skills to the test by entering orienteering competitions.

Serious hikers should learn how to navigate with compasses and topographic maps. This is called orienteering. Topographic maps have information about elevation and landscape, such as plant life. People can figure out where they are by matching the surrounding landscape with the information on the map. A compass is another useful tool. It has a magnetized needle that always points north. Hikers use a compass to know which direction they are facing and to guide them toward their destination.

A GPS device can be a helpful navigational tool in areas with no cell service.

It takes time to develop orienteering skills. Global positioning system (GPS) devices made for navigation of the outdoors are another option. These devices pinpoint someone's location by connecting with satellites. They have better coverage than cell phones. However, GPS devices also require batteries. If using one of these devices, hikers should make sure to bring extra batteries or a portable charger.

TREATING WATER

Hikers and campers should never drink directly from natural sources of water. Streams, rivers, and lakes can host bacteria, parasites, or viruses that make people very sick. Even clear water can be dangerous to drink.

Water filters can be used to make water safer to drink.

People should bring water with them. However, water is heavy. It may not be possible to carry all the water one needs during a long backpacking trip. For long trips, people should know how to treat water. There are many ways to do this. People should select clear, flowing water as a water source. Cloudy, still water is more likely to have germs.

Boiling water for five minutes kills all the germs in the water. But it is time-consuming and can take a lot of energy to start a fire and wait for the water to boil. Another option is to use a water filter. This device can remove particles and some disease-causing germs from water. Water filters can be bulky and difficult to carry. They also cannot filter out viruses.

Chemical tablets can be put in water to kill germs. However, they do not kill large parasites. They also change the taste of water. Hikers and backpackers should bring more than one way to treat water.

HYGIENE

Toilets are not always available on hiking or camping expeditions. People should know how to take care of their hygiene when spending long periods of time outdoors. They should know how to safely relieve themselves in nature. Bathing and taking care of other hygiene needs while outdoors takes planning and practice.

Some campgrounds have showers or restrooms.

Location is important when relieving oneself outdoors. It should be done at least 200 feet (61 m) away from water sources, campsites, and trails. Human waste can spread disease. Improper techniques can cause waste to enter waterways. It is dangerous for animals and people to drink contaminated water. When choosing a location to relieve themselves, people should go to less traveled areas. They should not return to the same place to relieve themselves in order to prevent damage to the landscape. Urine can harm plant life. People should urinate on gravel or rocks instead of vegetation.

Hikers and campers can reduce their use of toilet paper by using natural materials, such as nonpoisonous plant leaves. Woolly lamb's ear is one option.

Hikers and campers need to know how to safely dispose of waste. In some parks, people are required to pack out their waste to prevent harm to the environment. They should bring toilet bags to carry waste in a sanitary way. In other parks, hikers and campers can prepare and use a cathole. People use a trowel to dig a small hole in the ground. The hole should be about 6 to 8 inches (15 to 20 cm) deep. People squat over the hole to relieve themselves. It can be difficult to balance on uneven ground. People can hold onto a tree for support. They can also rest the backs of their legs on a fallen log to help with balance. Waste should be buried afterward. Biodegradable toilet paper can be buried in the cathole. But other toilet papers and feminine hygiene products must be packed up in plastic bags and disposed of outside the park.

A small shovel is necessary to bury waste.

After relieving themselves, people should clean their hands with hand sanitizer. They can also bring biodegradable soap that has a minimal effect on the environment. Other hygiene products to pack include natural toothpaste and baby wipes.

Campers and hikers should use hand sanitizer after relieving themselves as well as before cooking or eating.

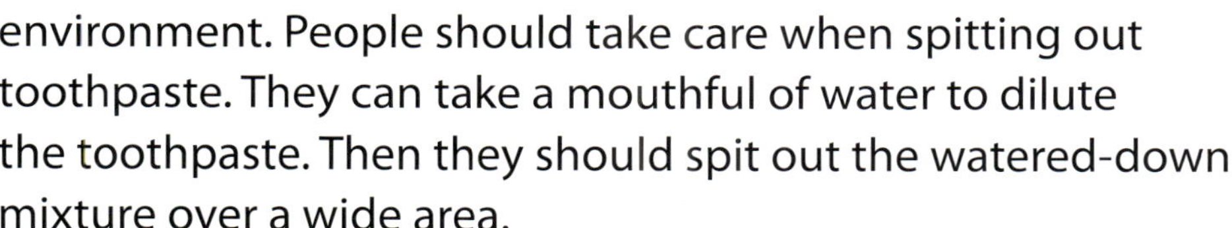

Campers should remember to leave no trace when they are brushing their teeth. Natural toothpastes are better for the environment. People should take care when spitting out toothpaste. They can take a mouthful of water to dilute the toothpaste. Then they should spit out the watered-down mixture over a wide area.

People do not need to bathe every day when they are camping. But on long camping trips, they will need ways to keep clean. A quick swim in a river or lake will rinse off dirt and grime. Soap should not be used in natural water sources. Even biodegradable soaps can contaminate the water. Sponge baths are another option. This should be done at least 200 feet (61 m) away from water sources

and campsites. To bathe this way, people bring water, biodegradable soap, and a cloth or sponge. They use the cloth or sponge to scrub themselves with soapy water. When they are finished, a quick-drying towel should be used to dry off. Hikers and campers can also use baby wipes to clean themselves. These need to be packed out for proper disposal. People can use unscented dry shampoos to keep their hair from getting greasy.

Campers need to know how to clean their dishes. They need a large container that they can fill with water. They can add a few drops of biodegradable soap to the water. Dishes are scrubbed clean in the container and left out to dry. Campers need to carefully dispose of the soapy water. The water will smell like food, which can attract wildlife. They should prepare a cathole away from the campsite and water sources. A pot lid or strainer should be used to collect food bits while the water is poured into the cathole. Leftover food should be thrown away in garbage bags. The dishwater is then buried to prevent animals from smelling it.

The amount of time it takes clothing to dry depends on weather conditions and clothing material.

On long camping trips, people will also need a way to do their laundry. Socks and underwear are the most important clothing items to keep clean. It is important to have several items of dry clothing when doing laundry because it will take time for clothes to air-dry. People should wash their clothes only on sunny days to reduce drying time. They will need two large containers, water, and biodegradable soap to do laundry. First, they pour water into both containers. They add a little bit of soap to one of the containers. Then, they scrub their clothes in the soapy water. After wringing out as much water from the clothes as they can, the clothing should be rinsed in nonsoapy water to get rid of any remaining suds. Excess water is wrung out again and the clothing can be hung in the sun to dry.

Water used to wash clothes has to be disposed of carefully. It should be dumped far from campsites and water sources. People should also get rid of the water over a wide area. That way soap is not concentrated in a single spot.

FIRE SAFETY

Many people enjoy sitting around a campfire during their camping trips. However, an improperly made fire can be dangerous. Campers should always check whether a campfire is allowed. Some areas never allow campfires. In other places, fire bans are put in place during periods of dry, windy weather.

Many national parks and forests have fire danger signs that tell visitors about the current fire risk. Visitors may not be allowed to start campfires during high-risk wildfire conditions.

Some campgrounds have established firepits. If a firepit is provided, that is the only place where campers should start a campfire. In the backcountry, campers may need to build their own fire ring. They should dig a shallow pit and line the bottom with sand or gravel. A fire ring should be made only in places where there are no low-hanging branches or dry brush. These materials could cause a wildfire if they are accidentally ignited. Similarly, campers should make sure that their tents and gear are located at least 15 feet (4.6 m) away, upwind from the fire area. Campers should never leave a fire unattended. A change in the wind could cause the fire to spread. People should be prepared with a bucket of water to put out a fire before it gets out of control.

Check campground rules and weather conditions before starting a campfire.

A good campfire spot is clear of low-hanging branches, dry leaves, or other materials that could accidentally catch fire.

For a visit to a campground, people should purchase packages of treated campfire wood. They should never bring wood from home. Wood from other places may carry insects that are not native to the campground. These insects can damage the landscape. Campers can also collect firewood around a campsite. However, they should collect only downed branches and sticks. They should not pull branches or bark from living trees. Standing dead trees are homes for wildlife and should not be disturbed.

DID YOU KNOW?

Dirt or sand should not be used to extinguish a campfire. Coals may continue to burn after being buried. Wind may uncover the burning coals and start a wildfire.

Hickory is a popular wood for campfires. It produces little smoke and its flames are hot enough to cook on.

It takes three types of wood to start a campfire. These are tinder, kindling, and fuel. Tinder is small twigs, dry grasses, or dry pine needles. Kindling refers to narrow sticks or branches. Large pieces of wood or logs are fuel. To start a fire, campers

should make a loose pile of tinder. Adding paper or a fire starter to this pile will make it easier to light. Once the tinder is burning, pieces of kindling can be added. The large pieces of fuel are added last. Wet wood burns slowly, but it is hard to ignite. Wet wood also produces a lot of smoke.

Wood fuel should be kept upwind of a campfire to help prevent campfires from growing out of control.

COOKING AND EATING OUTSIDE

Boiling, frying, and grilling foods are possible on a campfire. But using a campfire to cook can be challenging. The heat of the fire is difficult to control, which can result in foods cooking unevenly or burning.

For best results when cooking on a campfire, people should wait until the flames have died down. Then, a heavy-duty pot or pan can be placed directly onto the hot coals or onto a grate over the fire. Soot will build up on the bottom of the pot while cooking. People can coat the outside of the pot with soap

Campers should make sure that cooking equipment is made from materials that can withstand open flames.

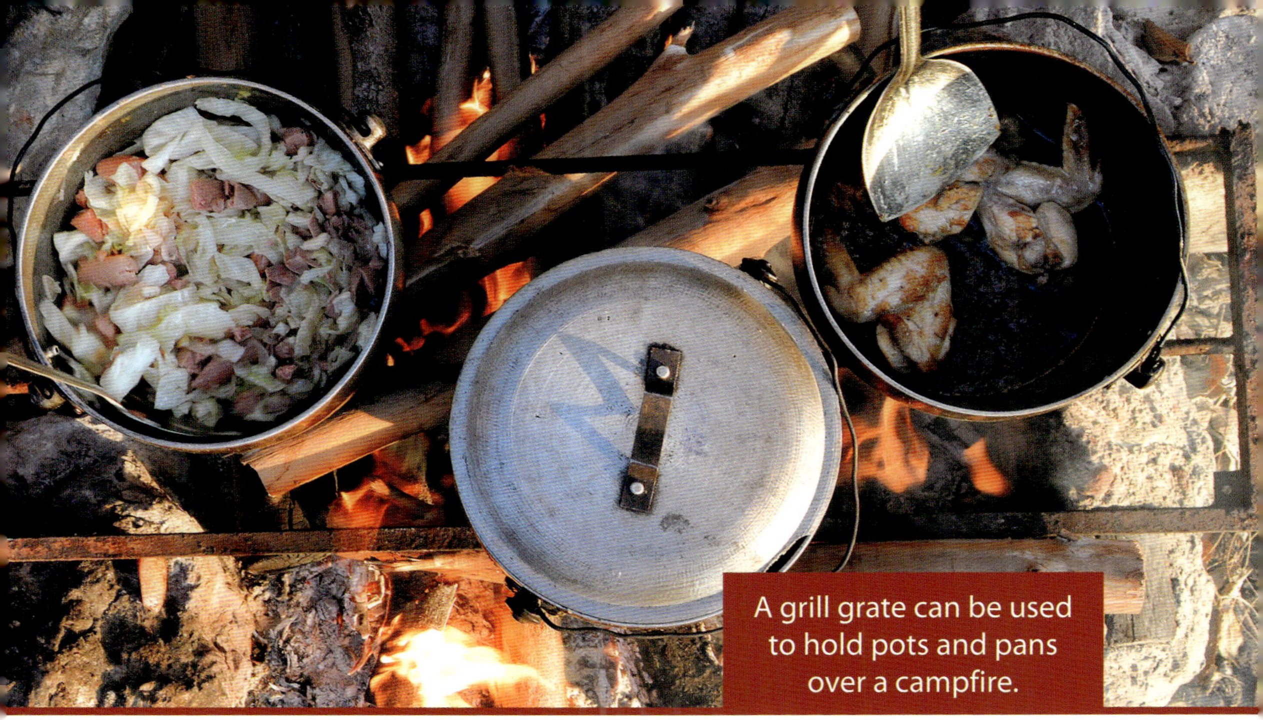

A grill grate can be used to hold pots and pans over a campfire.

before placing it over the coals. This helps prevent soot from sticking to the pot.

Some foods can be prepared without cookware. Chopped vegetables or meat can be wrapped in foil and placed directly onto hot coals. Small pieces of food cook more evenly. Some foods, including hot dogs and sausages, can be roasted on sticks over a fire.

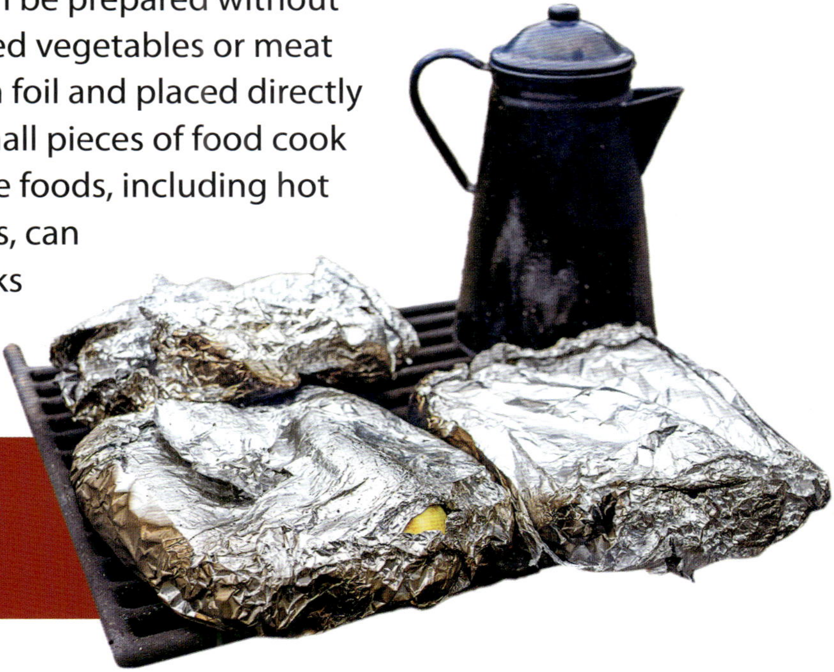

It takes about 25 minutes to roast vegetables over a campfire.

People can use special equipment to bake on a campfire. A Dutch oven is a cast-iron pot with legs. It can be placed over a small fire or camp stove. A lid covers the Dutch oven. Hot coals are put on the lid to make sure the oven is heated from all directions.

Camp stoves may be used instead of campfires. Stoves and fuel can be dangerous. Only adults who know how to use the equipment should cook on a camp stove. Camp stoves should never be used inside a tent. Using a stove inside a tent could cause deadly gases to build up. Extra fuel for the stove should also be stored carefully, outside of the tent and away from food.

Campers need to make sure their Dutch ovens are intended to be used over a campfire.

Campers must know how to properly store their food. Food and crumbs attract animals that could damage gear. Food that is not stored properly can also lead to wildlife encounters that are dangerous for both animals and people. During the day, food should not be left unattended. Food should never be kept in a tent at night. It can be stored in cars or food lockers.

DID YOU KNOW?

Some parks and campgrounds do not allow food to be stored in cars. Bears can learn to break into cars to access food. One woman from California reported that a bear got into her vehicle and ate an entire bag of dog food.

Parks with a known bear presence may have food lockers for people to safely store their food.

In bear country, extra safety precautions are necessary. Bear bags are used to store food. They are made of tough material that bears cannot rip open. These can be left on the ground. They can also be hung from a tree or bear pole using rope for additional security. Bear bags should be hoisted 10 to 15 feet (3 to 4.6 m) off the ground.

Rodents can chew through gear to get to food.

They should also be at least 4 feet (1.2 m) away from the tree trunk so they cannot be reached by climbing animals. Some parks require food to be stored in bear canisters, which are more secure than bear bags. These plastic containers have lids that need to be unscrewed to access the food.

Even the smell of empty food containers can attract bears.

Knowing basic first aid can be helpful if accidents occur while camping and hiking.

Campers and hikers should be prepared for the outdoors. They should make sure that they have packed all the gear they need. But emergencies can still occur even if people plan ahead. Campers and hikers need to know how to react or contact help when things do not go as planned.

Before going camping or hiking, people should tell friends and family members about the trip. They should let someone else know where they are going and how long they will be gone. That way if they do not return, a search and rescue team can be sent for help.

It is important to map out a route before setting off on a hiking trip.

Members of search and rescue teams are often trained volunteers.

Campers and hikers need to know how to call or signal for help in case of an emergency. Calling 911 works in places with cell reception, but people may not have service in the wilderness. If spending time in remote areas, people should have a satellite phone, personal locator beacon, or SOS device. These devices work even in places where there is no cell service. They use satellite connections or emergency radio channels to alert rescuers. It is important to make sure that the batteries in a cell phone or electronic emergency device stay charged.

A whistle or flashlight can also be used to signal for help. Three repeated signals is the universal call for help. For example, three shouts, three blasts of a whistle, or three flashes of light. These signals help rescuers locate a person who needs help.

In general, hikers and campers should call for help if someone is injured or sick and cannot get to safety. Some conditions that require assistance include uncontrollable bleeding, a broken limb, a head injury that causes dizziness or confusion, or a venomous snakebite. Dehydration, altitude sickness, hypothermia, and heatstroke may also require medical attention.

HOW SEARCH AND RESCUE WORKS

Search and rescue responses begin with a call. That call may come from an injured or lost hiker. Or it could come from someone who has reported that a hiker or camper has not returned from a trip. Rescuers investigate the case to find out as much as they can about the hiker's situation. Search and rescue teams are trained to respond quickly. Teams of responders may fan out over the area where the hiker is believed to be. They may use helicopters and trained dogs to help search. Approximately 97 percent of people are found within the first 24 hours of a search.

During an emergency, people should blow a whistle in a three-burst pattern until help arrives.

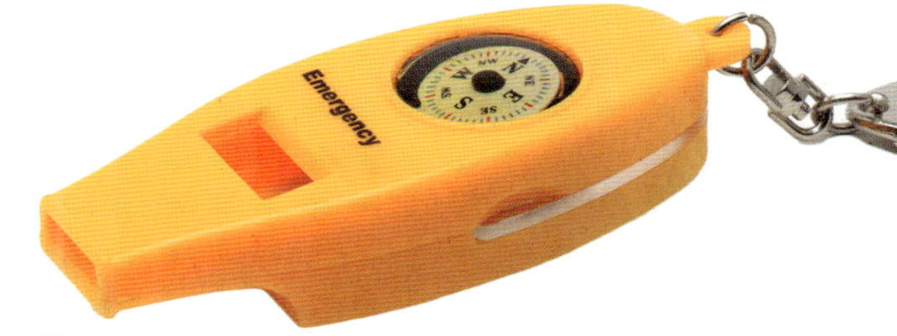

Steep, slippery conditions can make hiking difficult. They also increase the risk of falls. Severe falls require emergency attention. People who have fallen and are unable to get up should not be moved. Others will need to call for help. They should check the fallen person's breathing and give CPR if needed. They should also keep the person warm.

People can burn a signal flare to help search and rescue teams find their locations. Flares burn for about one minute.

Extreme weather can wash away tracks and scents, as well as make it more difficult for search and rescue teams to access remote areas.

People can call for help if they get lost and do not have the resources to spend the night. They should also call for help if weather conditions, such as a blizzard or lightning, have made travel unsafe. It is especially important to call for help if daylight is fading or weather conditions are worsening. Darkness and bad weather make it more difficult for a search and rescue team to do its job.

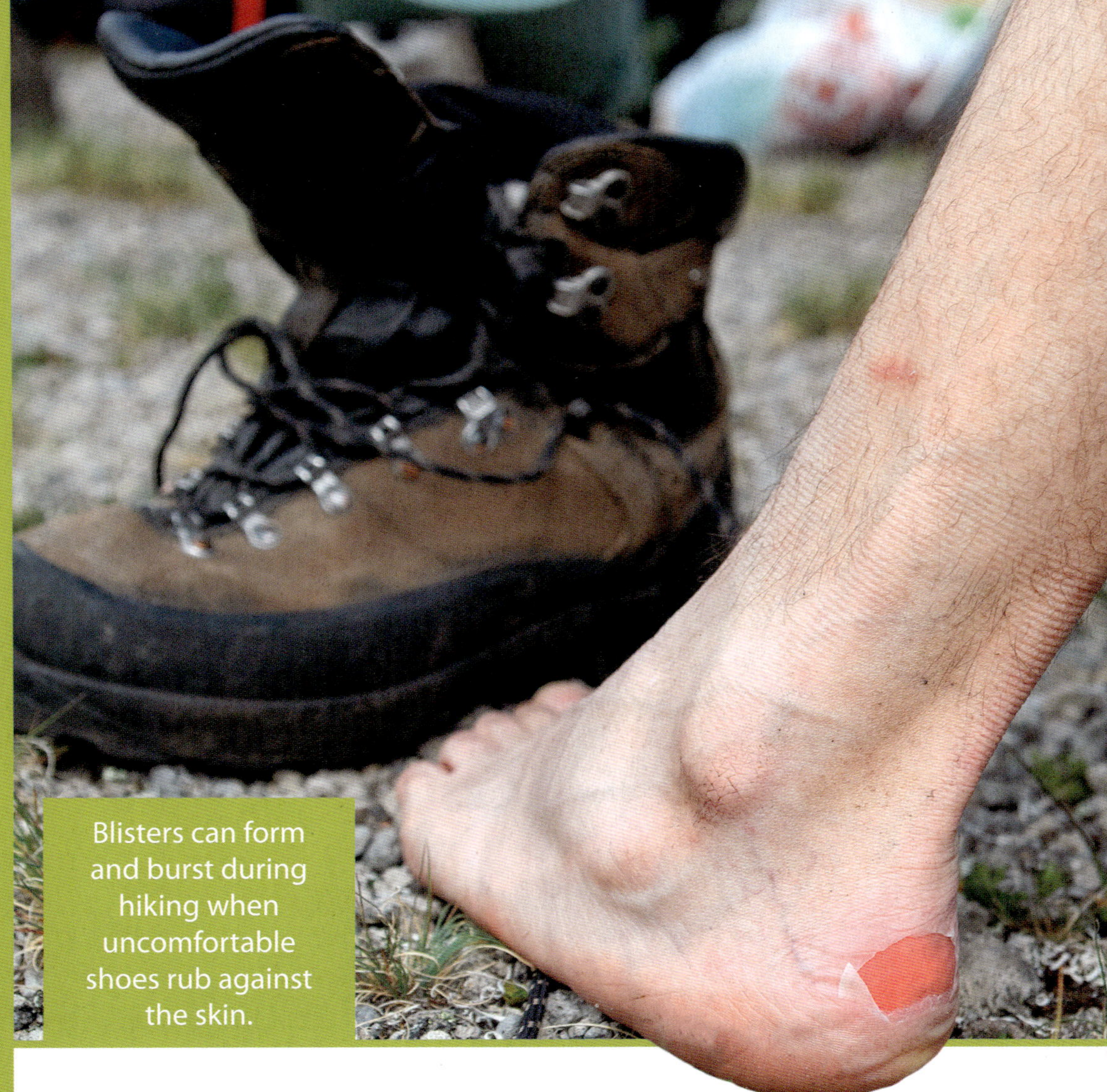

Blisters can form and burst during hiking when uncomfortable shoes rub against the skin.

TREATING MINOR INJURIES

Many camping and hiking accidents can be handled without calling for help. People should know how to use items in their first aid kits to treat minor injuries. For example, blisters are a common injury. They are more likely to occur when people are hiking in brand-new shoes. Hiking with wet feet can also cause blisters.

Moleskin is a special bandage that can be used to prevent or treat blisters. Moleskin is thicker than other bandages. It is also completely sticky on one side. Hikers can use moleskin on an irritated area to prevent a blister. If a blister has already formed, moleskin should not be placed directly on top of the blister. The adhesive could pull on the irritated skin and tear open the blister. Instead, a hole should be cut into the moleskin for the blister to fit through. The thick moleskin prevents other materials from rubbing against the blister. To prevent blisters in the first place, people can use second skin or liquid bandages. These products create a tough, protective layer.

Bandages and gauze can be used to cover a blister and prevent it from further irritation.

Animal bites and cuts that will not stop bleeding require medical attention. But minor cuts and scrapes can be treated with supplies in a first aid kit. People should clean their hands and wear clean gloves when helping someone treat a bleeding wound. To get a wound to stop bleeding, the victim or helper should apply pressure using clean gauze or a clean cloth. The wound should be elevated above the heart until the bleeding stops.

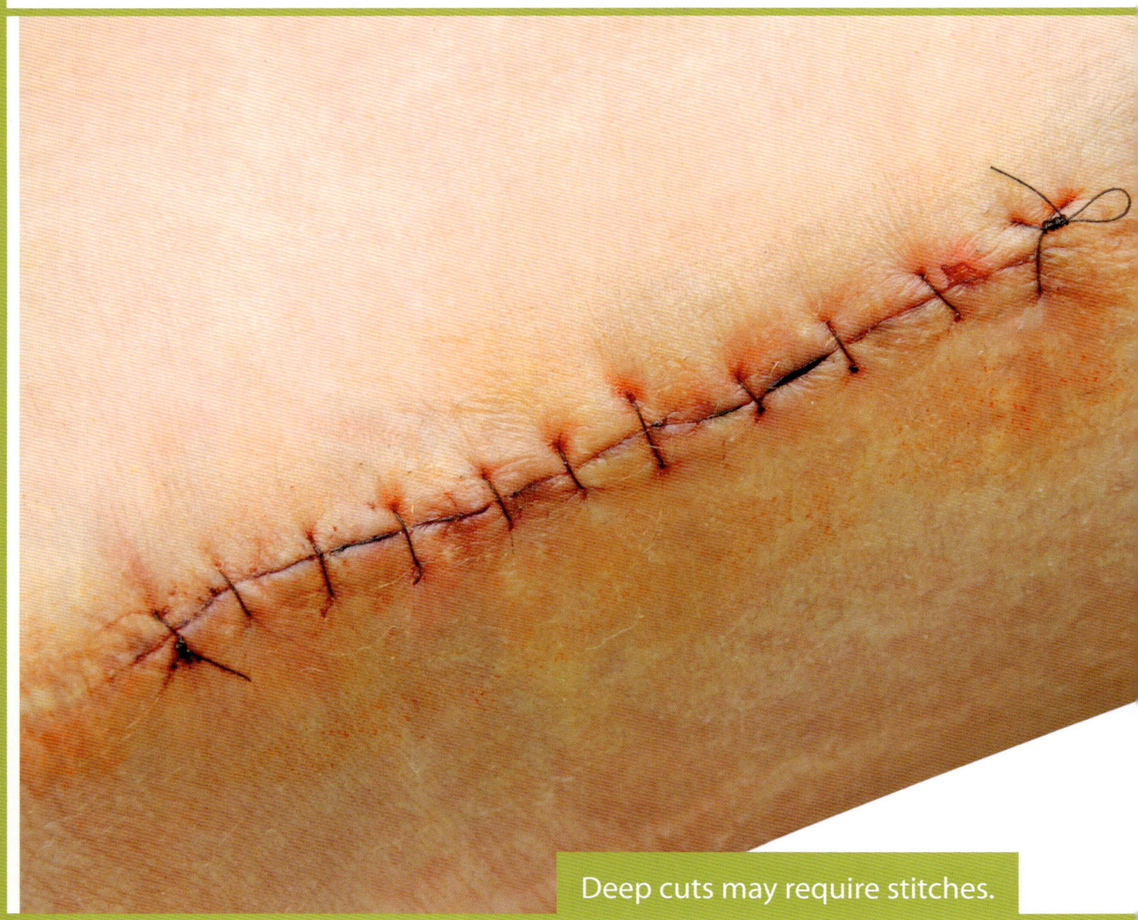

Deep cuts may require stitches.

Once bleeding has stopped, the wound should be rinsed with clean water. Any dirt or debris in the wound should be picked out with clean tweezers. Finally, an antibiotic ointment should be applied to the wound, and the injury should be covered with a bandage or taped over with gauze. If the bandage gets wet or dirty, it should be changed.

Hikers may experience injuries to joints called sprains. Ankle sprains are the most common sprains while hiking. They may occur when someone missteps or trips on a trail. To treat a minor sprain, hikers can apply an instant ice pack from a first aid kit to reduce pain and swelling. Next, they should use an elastic bandage to wrap the area snugly. For a severe

A sprained joint may swell and bruise.

sprain, they may need to make a brace out of a foam pad or clothing. A person can walk on a wrapped sprained ankle if it is not swollen and painful. Careful movements increase blood flow to the injury, which helps it heal. A hiking partner or trekking pole can provide additional support for the injured person to safely complete the hike or return to safety.

Sunburns are another common condition that hikers and campers experience. A sunburn can be treated with cold compresses, aloe vera gel, or sunburn ointments. People can take medicines containing ibuprofen to reduce pain from sunburns. They can wear clothes that cover the burns to prevent further exposure to the sun.

Doctors recommend that people use sunscreen that is at least SPF 60 when spending time outdoors.

Keeping a safe distance from campfires can prevent burns. People should not stand so close to a campfire that the heat becomes uncomfortable.

Campfires and camp stoves can also cause burns. Very large or severe burns require medical assistance. For minor burns, the victim should cool the area with treated water. Ice or ice packs can cause additional damage to the area and should never be placed on a burn. Petroleum jelly or aloe vera gel can help relieve the pain of a burn. So can over-the-counter pain medications. The burned area should be kept out of the sun.

ALTITUDE SICKNESS

Areas high above sea level have little oxygen. This can make it difficult to breathe. Hiking in mountainous areas can be tiring for this reason. People may experience altitude sickness because of the low amount of oxygen. Symptoms of altitude sickness include headache, dizziness, nausea, vomiting, tiredness, and shortness of breath. For most people, these symptoms occur at 8,000 feet (2,400 m) or more above sea level.

Someone experiencing mild symptoms of altitude sickness can remain at the current elevation while the body adjusts. For severe symptoms, people should return to a lower elevation and seek medical attention.

Gaining elevation slowly can help prevent altitude sickness. Mountain climbers should schedule in a rest day every third or fourth day.

People should prepare before heading to areas of high elevation. They should avoid strenuous physical activity while their bodies adjust to the altitude. Climbing slowly and drinking plenty of water help reduce the effects of altitude sickness. Hikers should return to a lower elevation if they begin to experience symptoms. People can also bring oxygen tanks to help them adjust to altitude changes.

HOT WEATHER CHALLENGES

Hikers need to be prepared for changing weather conditions. Different types of weather lead to different challenges when hiking or camping. The sun gives off harmful UV rays that can lead to sunburns. Continued exposure to UV rays also increases the risk of skin cancer. Sun protection should be worn even in the winter and on overcast days. Hikers should put on sunscreen half an hour before going outside and reapply it every two hours. Long sleeves and a hat with a brim also add protection. Sunglasses and hats help protect the eyes from the sun.

Sunglasses protect the eyes from UV rays.

Hot, sunny weather leads to other health challenges. It can cause hikers to overheat. They may suffer from heat exhaustion, which can develop into heatstroke if left untreated. Heatstroke is a life-threatening condition. Hikers should call 911 if they suspect someone has heatstroke. Signs of heat exhaustion include cool skin with goosebumps even though it is hot, heavy sweating, dizziness, muscle cramps, headache, and nausea. A person who is developing these

Sunburns can increase a person's risk of developing skin cancer in the future.

A person experiencing symptoms of heatstroke can be helped by placing cold cloths on the head, neck, and groin while waiting for medical help to arrive.

symptoms should try to find shade, rest, and drink fluids. Cold compresses can help cool the body as well. Heat exhaustion and heatstroke are more likely to occur in hot weather when a person is dehydrated or exercising. Humid weather also makes overheating more likely.

Wearing a hat helps prevent heat loss through the head.

COLD WEATHER CHALLENGES

Staying warm and dry is the major challenge for hikers and campers during the winter. People should pack extra layers, including a hat and scarf, when spending time outdoors in cold weather. A mask or gaiter protects the face from the wind and cold. People can wear gloves underneath mittens for extra warmth. The outer layer of clothing should be waterproof and windproof. Heat packs help keep fingers and toes warm. Skis and snowshoes may be necessary for travel in snow.

Winter campers require special gear. They should use a four-season tent that is built to withstand heavy snowfall and harsh winds. They should make sure to pitch the tent on sturdy ground in an area with protection from the wind. Campers should also make sure their tent site is away from tree limbs and dead trees. These may snap under the weight of snow. Other cold weather gear includes an insulated sleeping bag, a snow shovel, and a camp stove that functions in freezing temperatures.

Sunlight reflects off of snow, which can cause a person's eyes to become damaged by UV rays. This is called snow blindness. Symptoms include eye pain, headache, and vision issues. People typically recover from snow blindness after several days.

Snowshoes help people walk across deep snow without sinking.

One of the major health risks of spending time in cold weather is hypothermia. This condition occurs when a person's body temperature falls below 95 degrees Fahrenheit (35°C). Hypothermia can be deadly. It can cause organs and body functions to fail. Hypothermia is more likely to occur if a person's clothing is wet. Damp clothes pull heat away from the body. Strong winds can also make it difficult to stay warm.

Someone showing signs of hypothermia should be warmed slowly.

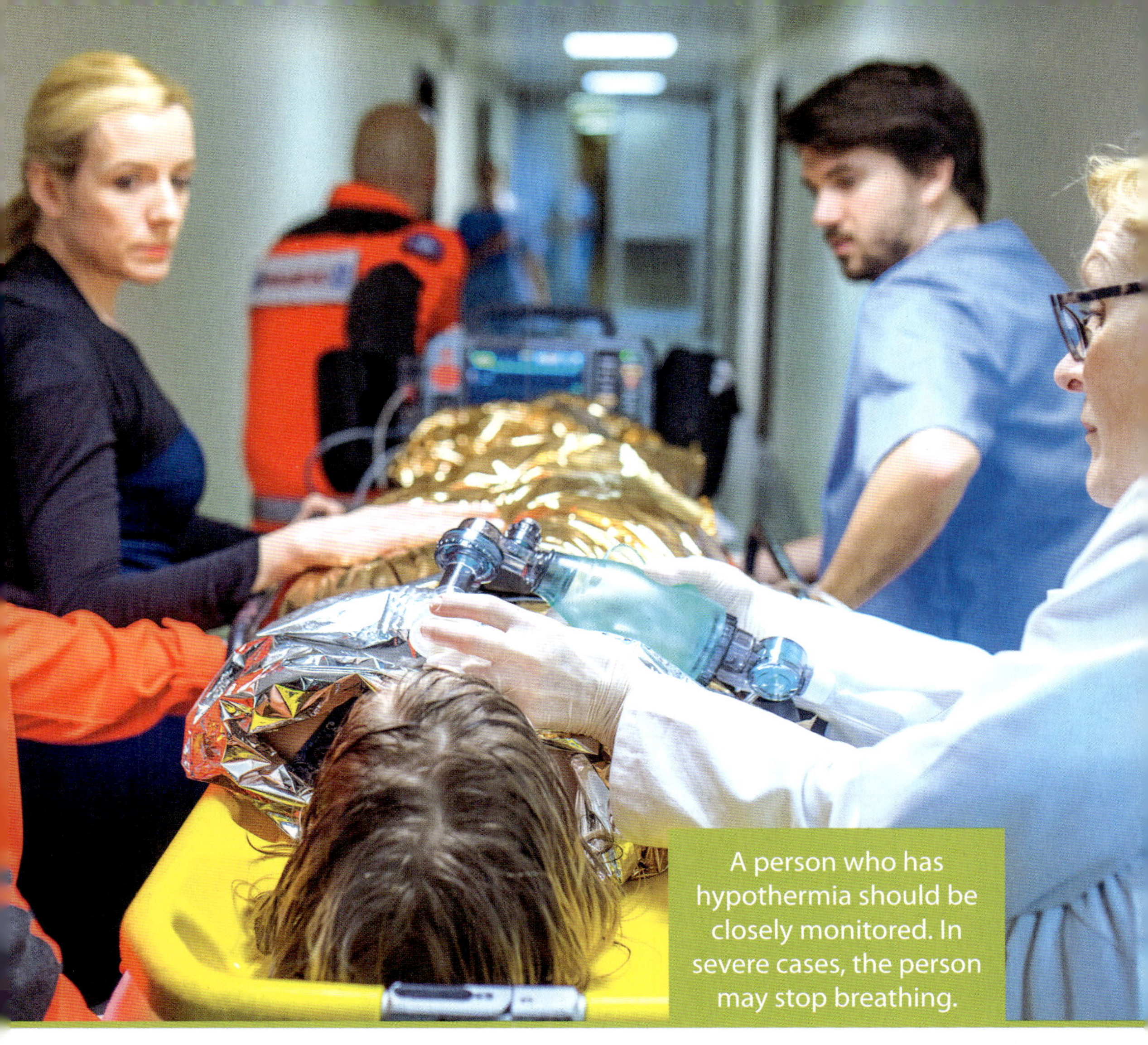

Symptoms of hypothermia include shivering, confusion, tiredness, and slurred speech. People showing any of these signs should be taken to shelter, warmed up, and kept awake. Wrapping them in an emergency blanket or sleeping bag will help if no shelter is available. Any wet or damp clothing should be removed. If possible, the person should be given a hot drink and some food.

STAGES OF FROSTBITE

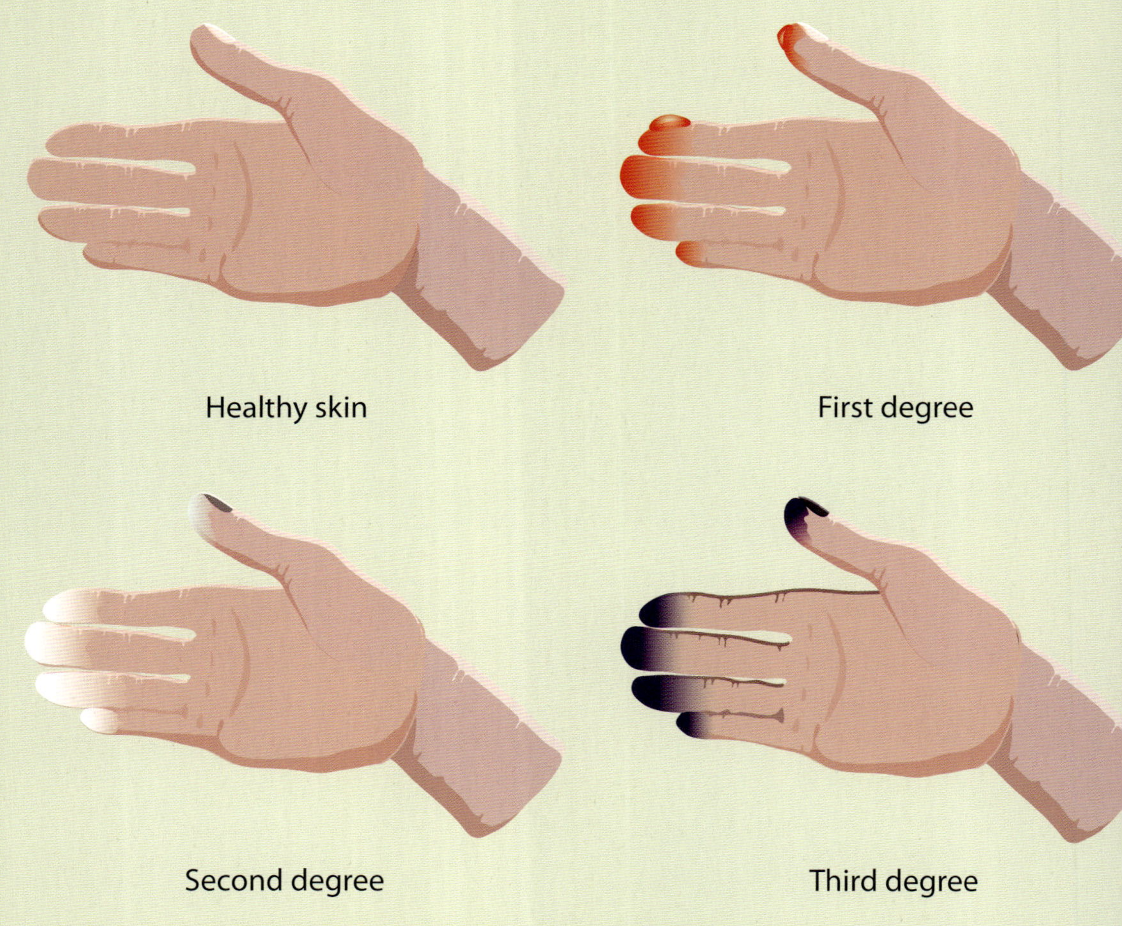

The skin changes color as stages of frostbite become more severe.

Frostbite is another cold weather condition. It occurs when skin tissues freeze. Frostbite is most common in the fingers and toes. Exposed skin on the face is also vulnerable to frostbite. In the early stages of frostbite, the skin is cold. People experience a prickling sensation and numbness in the area. They should seek shelter and warm the affected area before the frostbite becomes more severe. In severe cases of frostbite, skin may appear discolored. If skin has a purplish or black appearance, the tissue has died. The area may need to be removed by a medical professional.

Winter weather conditions can make it difficult to travel. Blizzards greatly reduce visibility. The strong winds and blowing snow can cause someone to suffer from hypothermia

or frostbite. If hikers get caught in a snowstorm, they should seek shelter and stay put until it is over. They may need to dig out a snow cave or snow trench. They can then cover the opening with an emergency blanket or tarp.

Snowy conditions can also cause avalanches. An avalanche is a mass of snow and ice that falls down a slope or cliff. They are most

FROZEN LAKES

During the winter, people may venture onto frozen lakes for hiking or ice fishing. This can be dangerous if the ice is not thick enough. Ice that is 4 inches (10 cm) thick is strong enough to support a person. Before hikers step onto the ice, they should tap it with a trekking pole. If it makes a hollow sound, the ice is not thick enough to support a person. Clear ice is stronger than white or discolored ice.

Hikers should pay attention to their surroundings when hiking in the snow. A treeless slope may be a sign of previous avalanches in the area.

likely to occur on steep hills after heavy snowfall. Avalanche forecasts give hikers information about how likely an avalanche is. Hikers should check the forecast before setting out on a hike. They should also be aware of their surroundings and stay away from steep hills. Even a small hill can produce a deadly avalanche. Hikers should also make sure they are not walking underneath a slope where snow may fall on them. They should stay alert for signs of an avalanche, such as cracking or thumping sounds.

RAINY WEATHER CHALLENGES

Rainy weather can create conditions that make it unsafe for camping and hiking. Heavy rainfall can lead to flash floods. This is one reason why campers should not set up tents right next to rivers or streams.

Hiking in the rain can increase the risk of slipping and falling.

Heavy rains can loosen soil and increase the risk of rockslides and landslides. These disasters are rare but can be deadly. Hikers should always stay on the trail, away from unstable areas.

A hiker stands under trees that were carried into a canyon by a flash flood.

Debris from landslides can travel at speeds of 35 miles per hour (56 kmh).

It is dangerous to be outdoors during a thunderstorm. If possible, campers and hikers should seek shelter indoors if a thunderstorm is approaching. They can take shelter in a car. An open pavilion or a tent is not safe. If they cannot get to shelter, they should find a ditch or low spot that is far away from tall trees, poles, or metal objects. People should spread out and crouch with their heads lowered until the storm moves on. This reduces the chance of getting struck by lightning.

CROSSING STREAMS

Streams and rivers can be challenging obstacles, especially if the water is deep, fast moving, or filled with rocks and other hurdles. Before crossing, hikers should make sure there is a safe place on the opposite bank. They can throw rocks into the water in several places to judge depth. They can throw in a stick to test water speed. If a stream or river crossing seems dangerous, hikers should turn around.

Campers and hikers should double bag their trash so that it does not attract wild animals.

DANGEROUS ANIMALS

Hikers and campers can admire wildlife from a distance, but they should avoid close encounters. All wild animals can be dangerous. They may carry diseases, such as rabies. They may attack people when stressed.

Bats are one type
of animal that
may carry rabies.
Animals with young
should be given
additional space.

People can reduce dangerous encounters. Many animals are attracted to strong odors. Hikers and campers should avoid strong-smelling soaps and hair products. They should never leave food or garbage out where animals could get into it.

Keep bear spray easily accessible when traveling in areas where bears are common.

Bears may be common on some hiking trails and in some campgrounds. Bear attacks are rare, but hikers and campers still need to be prepared. To avoid surprising a bear, people should make noise. Hikers or campers heading into bear territory should also carry bear spray. Bear spray does not work the same as bug spray. It is not applied to the skin. It is made of red pepper oil that irritates the eyes and lungs. Bear spray is used when a bear is about to attack. The spray has a limited range. Most sprays work at a distance of 25 feet (7.6 m). It should be aimed below the head of a charging bear. That way the bear will run into the mist from the spray.

	Black bear	Grizzly bear
How people should respond when approached	Raise arms, yell loudly, make as much noise as possible	Talk to it calmy, avoid eye contact, back away slowly
How people should respond when attacked	Use bear spray, fight back	Use bear spray, play dead, stay on the stomach, protect the back of the head

Hikers and campers should know how to react to bears in order to stay safe. The safest course of action differs depending on the type of bear.

Black bears and grizzly bears are common bears in the United States. These animals have different hunting habits. People will need to react differently depending on the type of bear they encounter. In both cases, people should not turn their backs and run away. Bears chase fleeing animals. People should use bear spray if the bear charges. They should make themselves look as large as possible if a black bear approaches. They should raise their arms and make as much noise as possible. If this does not scare the bear away, people should fight back. Attacks should be concentrated on the black bear's eyes and nose.

Grizzly bears are larger and more dangerous than black bears. In a grizzly encounter, a hiker should stay calm and avoid eye contact while slowly backing away. If a grizzly bear attacks, people should play dead. They should cover the backs of their heads and necks with their hands and remain on their stomachs until the grizzly loses interest.

Grizzly bears can weigh more than 700 pounds (318 kg).

A cougar is also referred to as a mountain lion, puma, or panther.

Other large animals may be a threat to campers and hikers. Many animals are more active close to sunrise and sunset. Avoiding activity during these times can reduce the chance of a dangerous encounter. If people run into a predator such as a cougar, they should not run away. They should make loud noises and try to appear as large as possible. They should back away slowly.

Even animals that are not predators can be dangerous. Large grazing animals, including bison, moose, and elk, may charge at people if they feel

POISONOUS PLANTS

It is not just animals that pose a danger to hikers and campers. Some plants are poisonous. Flowers such as daffodils and water hemlocks are toxic and should not be eaten. Other plants, including poison ivy, poison oak, and poison sumac, secrete sap that irritates the skin. People should be able to identify these plants so they can avoid them. Poison ivy has three leaves that may be green or reddish. Poison oak also has three leaves, but the leaves are rounded. Poison sumac is a tall shrub with green berries. Each of its leaves is a cluster of seven to 13 leaflets.

threatened. Bison have harmed more people than any other animal in Yellowstone National Park. People should stay far away from wild animals and never chase or scare them.

People may encounter snakes when they are camping and hiking. Many snakes are not venomous, and snakes generally bite only when disturbed. Hikers should use caution if they see a venomous snake or a snake they cannot identify. They should back away slowly and give the snake space. If bitten by a snake, people should stay calm and limit movement. High levels of activity cause venom to be absorbed more quickly in the body. People should clean the snakebite and seek medical attention.

Emergency responders located and transported a hiker who had been bitten multiple times by a rattlesnake.

Applying bug spray makes it less likely that insects will bite a person.

DANGEROUS INSECTS AND ARACHNIDS

Though small, insects, along with spiders, ticks, and scorpions, can be dangerous creatures. Some carry deadly diseases. Others may sting or inject venom that may require medical attention.

Mosquito bites can be itchy. But mosquitoes are also pests because they can carry diseases like West Nile virus (WNV), dengue, and Zika virus. WNV is one of the most common diseases transmitted by mosquitoes in the United States. Symptoms of WNV include fever, headache, and rash. In severe

cases, someone may experience a high fever and muscle weakness. WNV can be fatal. People who think they may have WNV should go to a doctor for diagnosis and treatment.

Hikers and campers can protect themselves from being bitten by mosquitoes or other insects. They should wear clothing that reduces skin exposure, such as long pants, long-sleeved shirts, and socks. They should also wear insect repellent. Mosquito nets offer protection for those who are sleeping outside of a tent. The location of a campsite is

There are several mosquito species in the United States that are known to carry diseases.

also important. Campsites that are breezy or are far from standing water will have the fewest mosquitoes. Citronella candles, mosquito-repellent lanterns, or bug zappers help limit mosquitoes near a campsite. Scratching mosquito bites can make it more difficult for them to heal. Applying an ice pack or anti-itch cream can offer relief.

Like mosquitoes, ticks are dangerous because they can carry disease. They transmit disease after biting and feeding on a human. Lyme disease is the most common tick-borne disease in the United States. An early sign of Lyme disease is

In addition to offering itch relief, ice packs can also reduce the swelling of mosquito bites.

a bull's-eye rash around the tick bite. Not everyone with Lyme disease will have a rash. Other symptoms include fever, fatigue, and headache. Lyme disease can cause long-term health issues, such as swollen joints and joint pain. People should see a doctor if they begin to experience flu-like symptoms after a tick bite.

After feeding, a blacklegged tick may swell to be more than three times larger than its unfed state.

Ticks need to feed on a person for 36 hours before passing on Lyme disease. For this reason, people should check themselves daily for ticks. They can remove the tick with tweezers and clean the affected area.

Bees, wasps, hornets, and yellow jackets may sting if threatened. Fire ants also have a painful sting. For most people, insect stings are painful but not otherwise serious. Other people may have an allergic reaction to an insect sting. They may have trouble breathing if the reaction is severe.

Fire ants in the United States are most common in the Southeast.

Yellow jackets may make their nests underground. Hikers and campers should pay attention to their surroundings and avoid disturbing the nests.

They should use an epinephrine auto-injector if they have one. This device has chemicals that help open the airways. If they do not have this device, they should seek immediate medical attention.

Hikers and campers should avoid anything that might be a wasp or hornet nest, including holes in the ground or in trees. If people get swarmed by stinging insects, they should run as far away as possible. They should use a fingernail or credit card to scrape any stingers out of the welts once they are in a safe location. Ice packs and pain relievers can help the discomfort.

Most spiders that hikers and campers encounter are not dangerous. But some types of spiders are venomous. Brown recluse and black widow spiders are common types of venomous spiders in the United States. Brown recluses are all brown. They can be identified by the dark-brown, violin-shaped patch on their bodies. They also have six eyes.

Brown recluse spiders are most likely to bite when they feel threatened.

Black widows are black with a red hourglass-shaped marking on their bodies. Both types of spiders are most common in the southern United States but live throughout the country.

Spider bites may cause difficulty breathing. They can also cause rashes, headaches, and blisters. Symptoms are most severe in children and elderly people. If people who have been bitten by a spider develop flu-like symptoms afterward, they should seek medical attention.

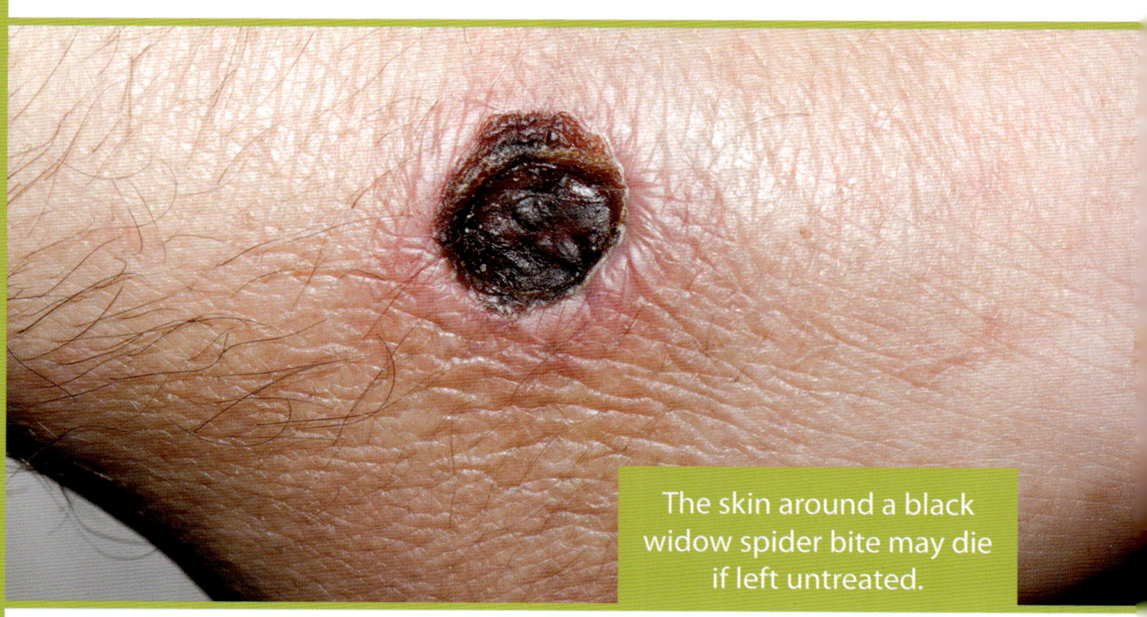

The skin around a black widow spider bite may die if left untreated.

    Scorpions are another dangerous creature. Almost all scorpions in the United States are found in the deserts of the Southwest. In an area with scorpions, campers should not leave shoes outdoors overnight. All gear should be shaken out to make sure nothing has crawled inside.

There are many places around the United States for people to go hiking and camping. National Scenic Trails are part of the National Park Service. Many of these trails extend through several states. Many national parks and national forests have designated campgrounds. They may also have trails for people to explore. However, people do not need to travel far to enjoy the outdoors. State and local parks offer many opportunities for people to experience nature.

Packing efficiently allows people to take more gear with them on camping trips.

HIKING AND BACKPACKING TRAILS

Hiking trails are common throughout the United States. Many websites and apps can help people locate nearby hiking trails. Hiking guidebooks contain maps and directions for hikes in a specific area. Local, state, and federal governments typically build and maintain trails. Sometimes, nonprofit organizations and volunteers do this work. National, state, and regional parks have hiking trails that vary in difficulty and length. Some hiking organizations offer hiking trips or backpacking expeditions led by professional guides.

The Highline Trail in Montana's Glacier National Park is part of the Continental Divide Trail.

National Scenic Trails are some of the most famous hiking trails in the United States. Eleven trails have this designation. The Appalachian Trail is one example. The Continental Divide Trail is another. This trail extends for 3,100 miles (4,989 km) and stretches from the southern border of New Mexico to the northern edge of Montana. This is a challenging, remote hike at high elevations. Only about 150 people complete a thru-hike of

DID YOU KNOW?

Some people challenge themselves to hike the Triple Crown. This means they have completed thru-hikes of the Appalachian Trail, the Continental Divide Trail, and the Pacific Crest Trail. Only about 600 people have accomplished this feat.

the Continental Divide Trail each year. The Pacific Crest Trail is another famous trail. It runs from Southern California to British Columbia in Canada. It takes about five months to hike the entire 2,650-mile (4,265 km) trail.

At more than 6,800 miles (10,944 km) in length, the American Discovery Trail is the longest hiking trail in the United States. It connects the East Coast to the West Coast, crossing 15 states and 14 national parks. It is maintained by the American Discovery Trail Society.

Mount Whitney is one point of interest along the Pacific Crest Trail. It is the highest point above sea level in the United States outside of Alaska.

NATIONAL PARKS

In 1872, Yellowstone National Park was established as the first national park in the United States. In 2022, there were 63 US national parks in 30 states and two US territories. These parks protect and preserve natural wonders. All national parks allow camping and hiking, though these activities may be restricted to established campgrounds and trails. Visitors need to buy a pass for day visits or make a reservation for a campsite at most national parks.

Visitors to Yellowstone National Park can hike on boardwalks to see famous sites such as the Grand Prismatic Spring.

National parks protect many kinds of landscapes, allowing visitors to have different hiking and camping experiences. For example, Glacier National Park and Yellowstone National Park have stunning views of the Rocky Mountains. Grand Canyon National Park and Zion National Park lie in the desert. Many people enjoy stargazing and camping underneath the clear skies of these parks. Everglades National Park in Florida allows visitors to hike through a wetland habitat.

Depending on the season, hiking and camping in national parks may require special gear.

People need to be prepared for the national park they visit. They may need to hike through snow in some parks, especially during the winter or early spring. Camping in the desert requires special gear. Visitors should have bear spray if they are spending time at a park in bear country.

NATIONAL AND STATE FORESTS

In addition to national parks, the US government also protects forests. The Forest Service was established in 1905 to manage these areas. This federal agency helps keep forests healthy and protects the natural resources there. While national parks preserve lands in their natural states, national forests may be used for logging, hunting, mining, livestock grazing, or fishing.

The Tongass National Forest in Alaska is the largest national forest in the United States.

There are 155 national forests and 20 national grasslands in the United States. Many states also have state forests, which are managed by state governments and serve similar purposes. National and state forests are almost always free to visit.

National forests may not have official campgrounds. But most allow dispersed camping. Visitors can use forest access roads to find remote places to park and camp. State forests may also allow dispersed camping, but visitors should

Superior National Forest has camping opportunities that range from rental cabins to dispersed camping.

Canoeing is a popular way to explore the Boundary Waters Canoe Area Wilderness in Minnesota. This wilderness area is a popular backcountry camping destination.

always check in advance. National and state forests also often have hiking trails.

WILDERNESS AREAS

Government agencies including the National Park Service and Forest Service also protect federal wilderness areas. There are 803 wilderness areas in the United States. These areas protect forests, mountains, deserts, wetlands, and beaches.

Desolation Wilderness in California is a wilderness area that is part of the Pacific Crest Trail.

Wilderness areas are meant to be as undisturbed as possible. Cars and other motor vehicles are not allowed in wilderness areas. The land cannot be used for mining or other commercial industries. However, activities such as camping and hiking are typically allowed. These locations are remote and hard to access. There are no roads in wilderness areas.

Camping in wilderness areas can be difficult, but the challenging experience is rewarding. With careful planning, campers can safely enjoy nature far from others. They will have great views of landscapes and observe undisturbed wildlife.

STATE PARKS, CITY PARKS, AND CAMPGROUNDS

National parks may be famous, but they aren't the only places for people to enjoy the wilderness. State parks, city parks, and private campgrounds also offer opportunities for hiking and camping. These parks and campgrounds often offer places to swim, fish, hunt, cycle, and watch birds, as well as places to camp and hike.

The United States has nearly 6,800 state parks that are managed by state governments. Most people live within driving distance of a state park. These parks also tend to be less busy than national parks, so visitors may not need to make reservations far in advance. They should still check the availability of campsites when planning a camping trip, though.

State parks often have visitor centers that can provide more information about campgrounds and hiking trails.

Visitors should always check the rules and regulations of the park they plan to visit, as they differ from park to park. Most state parks charge a daily fee. However, it is free to visit state parks in Arkansas, Illinois, Iowa, Kentucky, Missouri, Ohio, Pennsylvania, and Tennessee.

Central Park in New York City has many walking and cycling paths.

City parks are managed by local governments. These parks are typically much smaller than state parks. They are not likely to have campgrounds but usually contain playgrounds, picnic areas, and sports fields. They may also have walking, hiking, or cycling trails. Some are located on or near lakes and rivers and may permit boating, fishing, or swimming. These parks allow people living in cities and towns to enjoy the outdoors without traveling far from home.

Private campgrounds are an option for people who want to spend more time outdoors. These campgrounds are often located near cities or highways. It can be more expensive to camp on a private campground than in a state or national park. But these campsites may have Wi-Fi, swimming pools, laundry facilities, camp stores, miniature golf, playgrounds, and other helpful services and entertainment options. They also tend to have conveniences for RVs, such as large parking spaces, hookups, and dump stations. For these reasons, private campgrounds are a great option for people who are RV camping or trying out camping for the first time. They offer many of the services of a hotel while allowing access to nature as well. Many private campgrounds also have scenic trails, wildlife, and lakes or rivers to enjoy.

Spending time outdoors improves physical and mental health. People who do not regularly go camping or hiking may be nervous about these activities. But day hikes and RV camping are ways for beginners to spend more time in nature. With careful planning and the right gear, people can enjoy their camping and hiking experiences.

GLOSSARY

backcountry
A rural area or wilderness.

biodegradable
Able to be broken down by living things and natural processes.

calories
Units of energy contained in food.

chronic
Long-lasting or constant.

contaminate
To make dirty, infected, or unclean.

dehydration
A dangerous condition that occurs when the body does not get enough water.

durable
Able to withstand wear or damage.

endurance
The ability to withstand high levels of physical activity.

gear
Equipment.

hygiene
Practices that keep someone healthy and clean.

nutrient
A substance that living things need to be healthy and grow.

replenish
To fill up again.

spigot
A spout or faucet.

strenuous
Very difficult and requiring a lot of energy.

summit
The top of a mountain.

synthetic
Not natural; made by people through chemical processes.

terrain
The physical features of an area of land.

FURTHER READINGS

McKinney, Donna B. *Camping*. Abdo, 2020.

Perdew, Laura. *The Wildlife Watching Encyclopedia*. Abdo, 2024.

Towell, Colin. *Survival! A Step-by-Step Guide to Camping and Outdoor Skills*. DK, 2019.

ONLINE RESOURCES

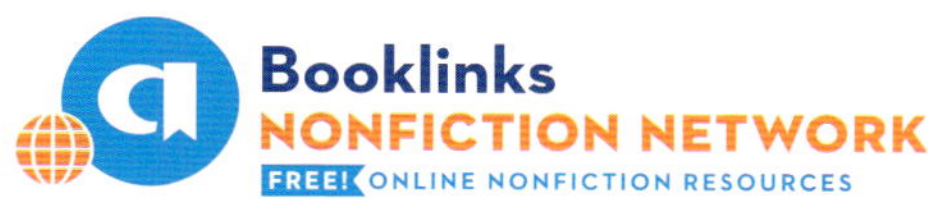

To learn more about camping and hiking, please visit **abdobooklinks.com** or scan this QR code. These links are routinely monitored and updated to provide the most current information available.

Cover Photos: Shutterstock Images, front (gear, tent); Billion Photos/Shutterstock Images, front (carabiners), back (pot, utensils); Alexander Ishchenko/Shutterstock Images, front (shoes, headlight); Hurst Photo/Shutterstock Images, front (map and compass); Maciej Bledowski/Shutterstock Images, front (rope); Kencana Studio/Shutterstock Images, front (water bottle); Olga Popova/Shutterstock Images, back (lantern)

Interior Photos: Shutterstock Images, 1, 5, 6, 8, 12–13, 14, 17, 20, 21 (top), 21 (bottom), 23, 28–29, 31, 32, 33, 35, 36, 38, 39, 40, 48, 53, 54–55, 55, 56, 57, 61, 72, 73, 74, 75, 78, 80, 88, 90–91, 91, 94, 95, 96 (top left), 96 (top right), 96 (bottom), 96 (stop signs), 99, 101, 103, 106, 111 (top), 111 (bottom), 112, 114, 116, 117, 119, 123, 124 (top), 126, 127, 130, 134–135, 136, 141, 142, 145, 146, 153, 156, 158, 160 (left, right), 164–165, 165, 168 (bottom), 169, 179, 185, 186; Vera Petrunina/Shutterstock Images, 2–3, 68; Margaret Wiktor/Shutterstock Images, 4–5; Monkey Business Images/Shutterstock Images, 7, 98, 138–139; Karel Stipek/Shutterstock Images, 8–9; CoroImage/Moment/Getty Images, 10; New Africa/Shutterstock Images, 11; Ljupco Smokovski/Shutterstock Images, 15; Jordan Siemens/DigitalVision/Getty Images, 16–17; Jordan Siemens/Stone/Getty Images, 18; Ryan J. Lane/E+/Getty Images, 19; Zapylaiev Kostiantyn/Shutterstock Images, 22; Kampee Patisena/Moment/Getty Images, 24; Twenty47Studio/Moment/Getty Images, 25; Rebecca Smith/Moment/Getty Images, 26–27; Ansis Klucis/Shutterstock Images, 28; Iablonskyi Mykola/Shutterstock Images, 30; Rania Musharraf/Shutterstock Images, 34; Cavan Images/Cavan/Getty Images, 37; Alex Lukin/Shutterstock Images, 41; Dean Drobot/Shutterstock Images, 42; Matthew Connolly/Shutterstock Images, 42–43; Patrick Lienin/Moment/Getty Images, 44; iStockphoto, 45, 58, 63, 107, 110, 115, 121 (bottom), 125, 128, 137, 147, 149, 172; David Madison/Moment Mobile/Getty Images, 46–47; Volodymyr Dyrbavka/Shutterstock Images, 47; Ashley-Belle Burns/iStockphoto, 49; Mariia Boiko/Shutterstock Images, 50; Vereshchagin Dmitry/Shutterstock Images, 51; Daniel Grill/Tetra Images/Getty Images, 52; Predrag Milosavljevic/Shutterstock Images, 59; Alex Brylov/iStockphoto, 60; Nina Lishchuk/Shutterstock Images, 62, 89; Romona Robbins Photography/Image Source/Getty Images, 64–65; Larry Crain/iStockphoto, 66; Christina Horsten/Picture Alliance/Getty Images, 67; Yury Stroykin/Shutterstock Images, 69; Ross Ellet/Shutterstock Images, 70; Brian van der Brug/Los Angeles Times/Getty Images, 70–71; Red Line Editorial, 76; Ryan J. Lane/iStockphoto, 77; Eugene Moerman/Shutterstock Images, 79; Galyna Andrushko/Shutterstock Images, 80–81; KyleWolfe/RooM/Getty Images, 82–83; Kyle Ledeboer/Aurora Photos/Cavan/Getty Images, 84–85; Robert F. Bukaty/AP Images, 86; Joel Carillet/iStockphoto, 87; Alexander Denisenko/Shutterstock Images, 92–93; Juan Pablo Olaya Celis/Shutterstock Images, 93; Andriy Blokhin/Shutterstock Images, 97; Alex Staroseltsev/Shutterstock Images, 100; Sander van der Werf/Shutterstock Images, 102; Hero Images/iStockphoto, 104–105, 113; Wagner Campelo/Shutterstock Images, 108; Bozena Fulawka/Shutterstock Images, 109; Bryan Pollard/Shutterstock Images, 118–119; Sercan Samancii/Shutterstock Images, 120; Sylvia Sooyon/Shutterstock Images, 121 (top); Daria Nipot/Shutterstock Images, 122, 144; Alison Catchpole/EyeEm/Getty Images, 124 (bottom); Nelson Peng/iStockphoto, 129; Peter Zay/Anadolu Agency/Getty Images, 131; Kirill Skorobogatko/Shutterstock Images, 132; Patrick Poendl/Shutterstock Images, 133; Imgorthand/E+/Getty Images, 135; Antonio Guillem/iStockphoto, 139; Andrew Peacock/Cavan/Getty Images, 140–141; Liudmila Chernetska/iStockphoto, 142–143; Trisha Mcmillan/iStockphoto, 148; Roman Mikhailiuk/Shutterstock Images, 150–151; Ryan McGinnis/Moment/Getty Images, 152–153; Andrew Geiger/Photodisc/Getty Images, 154; Sycikimagery/Moment/Getty Images, 155; Igor Cheri/Shutterstock Images, 156–157; Cheryl E. Davis/Shutterstock Images, 157; Constance Mahoney/Shutterstock Images, 159; Volodymyr Burdiak/Shutterstock Images, 161; Anan Kaewkhammul/Shutterstock Images, 162; CHP Golden Gate Division Air Operations/AP Images, 163; Chutima Chaochaiya/Shutterstock Images, 166; Anastasia Kopa/Shutterstock Images, 167; Dr. Gary Alpert/Urban Pests, Integrated Pest Management/CDC, 168 (top); Pong Wira/Shutterstock Images, 170 (top); Dr. P. Marazzi/Science Source, 170 (bottom); DeepDesertPhoto/RooM/Getty Images, 171; Cheri Alguire/Shutterstock Images, 173; Tom Robertson/Shutterstock Images, 174; TravelAdventure/E+/Getty Images, 175; Inger Eriksen/Shutterstock Images, 176; Harrison Weinberg/Shutterstock Images, 177; Martina Sliger/iStockphoto, 178–179; Dan Thornberg/Shutterstock Images, 180, 180–181; stevedunleavy.com/Moment/Getty Images, 182; Jonathan Percy/Shutterstock Images, 183; Kristi Blokhin/Shutterstock Images, 184; Olena Yakobchuk/Shutterstock Images, 187

ABDOBOOKS.COM

Published by Abdo Reference, a division of ABDO, PO Box 398166, Minneapolis, Minnesota 55439. Copyright © 2024 by Abdo Consulting Group, Inc. International copyrights reserved in all countries. No part of this book may be reproduced in any form without written permission from the publisher. Encyclopedias™ is a trademark and logo of Abdo Reference.

Printed in China

052023
092023

Editor: Angela Lim
Series Designer: Colleen McLaren
Production Designers: Michael J. Williams and Karli Kruse

LIBRARY OF CONGRESS CONTROL NUMBER: 2022949210

PUBLISHER'S CATALOGING-IN-PUBLICATION DATA
Names: Hulick, Kathryn, author.
Title: The camping and hiking encyclopedia / by Kathryn Hulick
Description: Minneapolis, Minnesota: Abdo Reference, 2024 | Series: Outdoor encyclopedias | Includes online
     resources and index.
Identifiers: ISBN 9781098291327 (lib. bdg.) | ISBN 9781098277505 (ebook)
Subjects: LCSH: Camping--Juvenile literature. | Hiking--Juvenile literature. | Outdoor life--Juvenile literature. |
     Encyclopedias and dictionaries--Juvenile literature.
Classification: DDC 796.5--dc23